Dyslogic Syndrome

of related interest

Kids in the Syndrome Mix of ADHD, LD, Asperger's, Tourette's, Bipolar, and More!
The one stop guide for parents, teachers, and other professionals
Martin L. Kutscher MD
With a contribution from Tony Attwood
With a contribution from Robert R. Wolff MD
ISBN 978 1 84310 811 5 pb
ISBN 978 1 84310 810 8 hb

Autism, Brain, and Environment
Richard Lathe
ISBN 978 1 84310 438 4

The Complete Guide to Asperger's Syndrome
Tony Attwood
ISBN 978 1 84310 495 7

Disorganized Children
A Guide for Parents and Professionals
Edited by Samuel M. Stein and Uttom Chowdhury
ISBN 978 1 84310 148 2

Genius!
Nurturing the Spirit of the Wild, Odd, and Oppositional Child – Revised Edition
George T. Lynn
With Joanne Barrie Lynn
ISBN 978 1 84310 820 7

Dyslogic Syndrome

Why Millions of Kids are "Hyper,"
Attention-Disordered, Learning Disabled,
Depressed, Aggressive, Defiant,
or Violent – and What We Can Do About It

Bernard Rimland

Jessica Kingsley Publishers
London and Philadelphia

First published in 2008
by Jessica Kingsley Publishers
116 Pentonville Road
London N1 9JB, UK
and
400 Market Street, Suite 400
Philadelphia, PA 19106, USA

www.jkp.com

Library of Congress Cataloging in Publication Data
Rimland, Bernard, 1928-2006.
 Dyslogic syndrome : why millions of kids are "hyper," attention-disordered, learning
disabled, depressed, aggressive, defiant, or violent - and what we can do about it / Bernard
Rimland.
    p. cm.
 Includes bibliographical references and index.
 ISBN-13: 978-1-84310-877-1 (alk. paper) 1. Behavior disorders in
children--Environmental aspects. 2. Behavior disorders in children--Nutritional aspects. 3.
Behavior disorders in children--Physiological aspects. 4. Neurotoxicology. 5. Behavioral
toxicology. I. Title.
 RJ506.B44R56 2008
 618.92'89--dc22
                    2007019946

British Library Cataloguing in Publication Data
A CIP catalogue record for this book is available from the British Library

ISBN 978 1 84310 877 1

Printed and bound in the United States by
Thomson-Shore, Inc.

Contents

Introduction

This is a book about "lost children." It's about children who fail at school and at life. It's about children who commit crimes, and children who react to loving families with hostility or violence. It's about hyperactive kids, and children battling depression or bipolar disorder. But the first "lost children" I studied weren't criminals, or kids failing math, or depressed children, or children who climbed the walls or yelled obscenities at their moms.

They were children even worse off—they were autistic. Trapped in a world of their own, they cried, screamed, rocked, and hit. Many shrank from hugs, and lashed out if their parents tried to touch them.

And one of them was mine.

This was back in the 1950s. I was a young psychologist, well schooled in experimental psychology, statistics, and the measurement of individual differences. My training, however, did me no good when Mark, my first child, arrived.

Mark didn't just cry. He screamed as if in rage, hour after hour, so violently that he could hardly nurse. He hated being held. As he grew, he began rocking and banging his head against his crib. He stared into space for hours, and looked through, rather than at, everyone, including his mother and me, as though we were invisible. His first words, spoken at only eight months of age, were "spoon," "bear," "all done," and "come on, let's play ball." A few months later, he began to repeat nursery rhymes, radio commercials and questions, all spoken in an expressionless voice as if by a robot.

We had no idea what was wrong. Our pediatrician, who had been in practice for 35 years, was baffled as well. He had never seen or heard of such a child. When Mark was two, however, my wife put a name to his condition. She remembered having seen a description, in an old college textbook stored in a box in our garage, of autistic children—children who acted just like Mark. In that textbook I saw the word "autism" for the first time—five years after earning a Ph.D. in psychology.

But putting a name to Mark's problem didn't solve it. Neither did the chilling words in the books about autism that I tracked down at the library. Autism, all the books said, stemmed from damage done by cold, unfeeling parents who irreparably scarred their children's psyches. Mothers were the major culprits. The textbooks' authors, led by then-revered psychologist Bruno Bettelheim, uniformly blamed "refrigerator mothers," who, the psychiatrists were sure, were subconsciously rejecting their children. Bettelheim likened the mothers to guards in Nazi concentration camps, dedicated to oppressing those under their control.[1] Other authors varied the theme by blaming "smother mothers," who, the psychiatrists charged, refused to let their children be themselves.

The medical authorities writing these books were cruel and unsparing. I knew that, at least in our case, they were wrong. It was impossible to picture my loving, intelligent wife as an evil destroyer of children. And Mark's uncontrolled tantrums were apparent in the maternity ward, on the day he was born. How could a happy, loving new mother, ecstatic over the arrival of her child, subconsciously "smother" or "freeze" a newborn?

My questions initiated a personal and professional odyssey spanning nearly five decades. It began with my intensive search of the scientific literature, which led to the conclusion that autism was a biological disorder, rather than an emotional illness caused by bad mothering. My research formed the basis for my 1964 book *Infantile Autism: The Syndrome and Its Implications for a Neural Theory of Behavior,* which is credited with destroying the psychoanalytical myths about autism.[2] In 1979, just 15 years later, David Katz wrote that a revolution had taken place: "Ninety percent of the people in the field agree that Rimland's book blew Bettelheim's theory to hell."[3]

As my research into the roots of autism progressed, and expanded into other areas, such as schizophrenia, depression, and psychopathy, it became clear that the Freudians were dangerously deluded, and had seriously misled our culture. I learned that, contrary to what the textbooks said, and what our instructors taught, disorders such as schizophrenia, depression, and autism stemmed from brain dysfunction, not from faulty parenting, and that the years that parents and their children spent in psychotherapy were not only wasted but injurious.

Things have changed a great deal since that time, and the fact that major psychiatric disorders have biological underpinnings is now widely accepted. Today, parents of children with autism or schizophrenia don't hear, "It's your fault." But it took more than two more decades to overturn the "bad families cause mental illness" theories—theories that caused great harm to many thousands of parents wrongly scapegoated by the psychiatric establishment. Worse yet, these theories stopped us from discovering the real causes of autism and schizophrenia. Now, decades later, we are belatedly uncovering the biological roots of these problems, and finding new treatments for children once labeled as "hopeless."

From autism to dyslogic

What does my story about autism have to do with otherwise "normal" children who fail their classes, drive their teachers crazy, spend their days in a dark cloud of depression, or torment their parents with hyperactive or hostile behavior—or with children who rob their neighbors, rape their girlfriends, or shoot their classmates?

Everything—because today the parents of these children are victims of the same scapegoating my wife and I experienced nearly fifty years ago. When depressed children commit suicide, we wonder if their parents failed to give them enough support or attention. When school shootings occur, we blame parents for letting the tragedies happen. When we watch news stories about children who rape or rob or kill, we hear reporters ask, "How could parents raise such horrible children?" Not long ago, for instance, my local newspaper ran a story about a couple of teenagers breaking into a house, destroying the owners' property, and writing obscenities on the walls. A police officer, interviewed about the crime, said that one thing was obvious—the kids who did it had bad parents.

But the parents of troubled or dangerous children typically *aren't* bad people. I know, because I've met hundreds of them—and you have, too. They are, by and large, loving and dedicated and normal parents. Moreover, I've met and worked with dozens of doctors and researchers who are proving, beyond a doubt, that most "bad" children—much like autistic or schizophrenic children—suffer from toxic *physical* environments, often coupled with genetic vulnerability, rather than toxic *family* environments. As I'll demonstrate in this book, research clearly shows that the culprits primarily responsible for the dyslogical behavior of millions of America's children are not their parents, but rather the poor-quality food substitutes they eat, the pollutants in the air they breathe, the chemically contaminated water they drink, and other less well-known physical insults that cause malfunctioning brains and bodies.

Many of these children are labeled "hyperactive" or "attention-disordered." Some are labeled "conduct disordered." Some are labeled "oppositional." Thousands are labeled "depressed" or "bipolar." And many are simply dismissed as hopelessly warped or evil. They struggle at school, they struggle through life, and in their wake they leave a trail of misery—of disrupted and saddened lives. But it's not truly their fault, and it's rarely their parents' fault.

In fact, the parents of these children are often nothing short of heroic. They battle ceaselessly to find help for their sons and daughters, only to find blame where they expected to find hope. They spend thousands of dollars seeking medical advice, and come away with nothing more than often harmful and frequently useless prescription drugs, and condescending or accusatory lectures. Pediatricians tell them that their children can't be cured, but can only be medicated. Psychiatrists tell them that their children suffer from traumas stemming from family dysfunction, which just adds to these parents' feelings of shame and guilt.

But these parents, far from being the problem themselves, are scapegoats for problems that they did not cause, and cannot cure—at least, not until a revolution in our thinking occurs. I hope that this book will, at least in some small way, contribute to the beginning of that revolution.

In the following chapters I identify many of the biological culprits that play a major role in our epidemic of dyslogic—the brain cripplers placing America's children at risk for criminality, underachievement, learning disabilities, and failure. The data and case studies I present in these chapters show conclusively that most troubled or "bad" children suffer from biological disorders and desperately need biological interventions.

Even more important is the good news: *these disorders can often be prevented or effectively treated.* We can turn around the lives of many delinquents, hyperactive children, and school under-achievers and we can do it without either futile parent-blaming psychotherapeutic approaches or the use of harmful mind-altering drugs such as Ritalin or antidepressants. Toward that end, this book concludes with an action plan for parents and professionals who want to stop the dyslogic epidemic that has engulfed our children. By implementing these simple but crucial suggestions, we can begin to reverse this epidemic, before it can harm today's children and generations to come.

Notes

1   Bettelheim, B. (1967) *The Empty Fortress: Infantile Autism and the Birth of the Self.* New York: Free Press.

2   Rimland, B. (1964) *Infantile Autism: The Syndrome and Its Implications for a Neural Theory of Behavior.* New Jersey: Prentice-Hall.

3   Katz, D.R. "The kids with faraway eyes." *Rolling Stone*, 8 March 1979, 48–53.

PART I

The Dyslogic Epidemic

Why brain dysfunction is making so many of America's
children "dumbed down," depressed, disturbed, or
dangerous—and how we can solve the problem

CHAPTER 1

Overview: What is "Dyslogic?"

"It would have looked stupid if I pulled the gun and then didn't shoot him. I would have looked dumb."

—A 15-year-old who killed another boy after exchanging "trash talk" with him

You might not realize it, but *you* have a brain dysfunction. There is, almost undoubtedly, some part of your brain that malfunctions some or all of the time. Maybe you have trouble reading a map, balancing your checkbook, or remembering where you parked.

This brain dysfunction might stop you from being a truck driver or an accountant, but it won't stop you from being happy, getting a good job, or making friends. And it won't make you kill your spouse, beat your children, or shoot a driver who cuts you off in traffic.

But what if that brain dysfunction *did* drastically change your thinking and behavior? What if you couldn't think logically much of the time—couldn't make good decisions, plan for the future, remember the past correctly, learn new information easily, experience normal emotional reactions to life events, control violent impulses, learn from your mistakes, see another person's point of view, or understand the consequences of your actions?

In that case, your brain dysfunction wouldn't be a small inconvenience. It would cripple you, making situations that other people take in their stride—being quiet in school, controlling your temper, finding a job, having a successful relationship—difficult or even impossible. In

15

short, it would make you "dyslogical." It could also, very possibly, make you a danger to society.

For a person with such a brain dysfunction, every day is a struggle. Just as the color-blind person sees colors wrongly, the person with a serious brain dysfunction perceives reality poorly, and makes poor decisions based on those wrong perceptions. We have names and treatments for extreme cases of such dysfunction: schizophrenia, autism, alcoholic intoxication. But we fail to recognize the plight of individuals disabled by more subtle but still very dangerous cognitive defects—defects that prevent them, either consistently or sporadically, from thinking and acting logically.

> *A teenager guns down and paralyzes a jogger who refuses to give him his "rope," street slang for a gold chain. When a therapist asks the teen why he committed the crime, he replies, annoyed, "He could have given me his rope. I asked him twice."* [1]

In this book, I use the term *dyslogic syndrome* to describe the cognitive defects that lead children to commit illogical, destructive, and even dangerous acts. The term has its roots in a telephone conversation I had back in 1975 with John Wacker, a learning disabilities activist in Dallas, who called me to ask, "Do you have a few minutes? I'd like to discuss an idea with you."

John said, "I'm writing a paper in which I plan to introduce the learning disability community to a very important issue that nearly everyone has overlooked. The issue is that many learning disabled kids, who of course have well-known problems with reading, math, and spelling, also have a much more serious brain problem—a problem with reasoning. You ask a simple question such as 'Why did you do that?' and the answer you get is often weird. It shows a strange twisted logic. These kids can't think straight, and that's why they get into trouble so often."

John had put his finger on a problem ignored by most doctors and educators, but all too clear to parents raising learning disabled children: the fact that defects in learning and cognition, in addition to causing problems in school, often lead to serious behavioral problems.

Now, compiling his observations and research into a paper, he was seeking an appropriate name for this problem. I suggested "dyslogic syndrome," which he liked and used as the title of his seminal paper. John's paper went on to become one of the most-read papers of all time in the learning disability community.

When John Wacker wrote his original paper on dyslogic syndrome, he was intrigued by the high rate of dyslogical behaviors in children with learning disabilities. But continuing investigation led him, and many other researchers, including me, to a troubling conclusion: dyslogical thinking is common, not just in the learning disabled population but in the general population as well. Dyslogic is not merely a problem of children identified as learning disabled; it is a problem that affects millions of other children who are labeled as "defiant," "conduct disordered," "depressed," "oppositional," suicidal, angry, hostile, sad, anxious, delinquent, under-achieving, unmotivated, and a hundred other terms that overlook or downplay their brain dysfunction.

These children, like the learning disabled children described in the original "dyslogic syndrome" paper, are ill-served by a system that attempts to treat them with the wrong tools. We've tried for decades to combat irrational, illogical, and destructive behavior—what I refer to in this book as "dyslogic"—with psychosocial and sociological solutions. We hire school psychologists to counsel at-risk children. We sponsor mentor programs for children from dysfunctional or abusive families. We conduct programs to raise children's self-esteem, and to teach them to say "no" to drugs. We sponsor "Scared Straight" programs to turn troubled teens away from a life of crime. We offer delinquents and criminals intensive psychotherapy.

These are well-intentioned efforts—and with few, if any, exceptions, they are utter failures. As I'll demonstrate later in this book, statistics show that sociological and psychological interventions have almost zero success in rehabilitating criminals or troubled youths, or in preventing dyslogical behavior in either at-risk or typical children. Some interventions, in fact, actually make matters worse.

Why? As a researcher who has spent many decades studying the problem, I believe that most people trying to deal with dyslogical behavior are on the wrong track. By focusing almost exclusively on presumed psychological causes, these well-intentioned counselors, doctors, teachers, and social workers ignore a vast and growing body of scientific evidence showing that the problems of difficult or dangerous people stem largely, and perhaps in many cases totally, from biological malfunctions of their brains. The evidence I will outline in this book demonstrates—conclusively, I believe—that a significant proportion of the "crazy" behavior that we see in our society stems from brain dysfunction rather than from psychosocial ills.

Sally, a friend of mine, has a son named John who owns a PlayStation. Recently, several of John's favorite PlayStation games disappeared from his backpack. Sally heard through the grapevine that another boy, Derrick, was bragging to his friends about stealing the games.

A few days later, Sally's doorbell rang, and Derrick was on the front step.

"Is John here?" he asked. "I want to borrow one of his games."

"The kids in the neighborhood say you stole two of John's games," Sally said. "Is that true?"

"I didn't take them," the boy replied, innocently.

Then he thought for a minute, and said, "And I'll give them back if he'll loan me another one."

This child, who already has a minor criminal record, will undoubtedly plague our correctional system for decades to come. Counselors will almost certainly point to his single mother, or his rejection by his peers, as reasons for his behavior. But Derrick's real problem is cruelly clear: quite simply, he can't think clearly, and because he can't think clearly, he can't understand the moral implications or the real-life consequences of his actions. As a result, he will continue to alienate his friends, fail at school and at life, and cause trouble for society—at least until someone finds and treats the real causes of his disabling dyslogic.

Our failure to understand that dyslogical brains cause dyslogical thinking and behavior has devastating consequences, because no amount of psychosocial intervention can correct the distorted thoughts of a malfunctioning brain. Insight therapy can't save a child whose brain is too dysfunctional to have meaningful insights. Special education and behavioral therapy won't help a child whose brain functions too poorly to follow any rules. And no amount of government funding for midnight basketball, pregnancy prevention programs, or counseling can truly aid a brain that's malnourished, burdened by toxins, or impaired by pre- or post-natal exposure to drugs or alcohol.

Why, then, do we ignore the role of brain dysfunction when our children can't read or write, can't follow rules, and can't think straight—or when they rape their dates, set fires, or kill their classmates?

The answer is simple: decades of psychoanalytic psychiatry and sociological theorizing have conditioned us to blame the problems of troubled children on outside forces, from bad moms and dads to bad societies. We have been misled into overlooking the very source of maladaptive behavior and thought: the brain itself. We tend to imagine thinking as a disembodied process that magically stems from a noncorporeal "mind" that can be perturbed only by psychic, not biological, misfortune.

That's a huge mistake, because thinking, just like breathing or perspiring, is a bodily function. All of your thoughts and feelings, no matter how lofty or deranged, stem from chemical and electrical signals in your brain, and how well you behave depends to a great degree on how well your brain works.

That's not to say, of course, that the brain doesn't react to what happens in the world around it. But a healthy brain reacts logically, while a dysfunctional brain reacts irrationally. A child with a healthy brain reacts to a failed geometry test by feeling sad for a few hours. A child with an unhealthy brain may react by shooting his parents, or planting a pipe bomb in his geometry class, or hanging himself from the backyard swing set.

Just as we tend to overlook the brain's role in behavior, so do we overlook another fact: the biological process of thinking is easily disrupted. The brain, the body's most complex organ, is also the most delicate, making it an easy target for toxins and other insults. Cut the supply of nutrients to the brain, choke off its oxygen supply, lower its supply of glucose, or pollute it with heavy metals or chemicals, and it malfunctions. When the lungs don't work properly, emphysema or respiratory failure results. *When the brain doesn't work properly, dyslogical thinking results.* The brain is the root of all behavior and emotion, and when it is flawed, the thoughts and actions it produces are flawed, often dangerously.

One concept that's crucial to understanding brain dysfunction, and the dyslogical behavior that results, is "body burden." In some cases, a single insult (massive exposure to toxic solvents, for instance) can cause permanent brain dysfunction. More often, however, the cumulative effect of repeated insults pushes a brain into dyslogic. A child with an innate genetic vulnerability or a mildly elevated lead level may still be able to behave well, sit quietly in class, and control his impulses. Feed him a diet deficient in vitamins and minerals, however, and his brain becomes still more compromised. Add more insults—for instance, load his brain with the artificial chemicals found in junk foods, pesticides, and household chemicals—and he becomes a prime candidate for learning disabilities, hyperactivity, depression, or antisocial behavior.

But is brain dysfunction, in and of itself, enough to cause dyslogical or even criminal behavior? In many instances, yes. Millions of children from good, loving, intact families become robbers, rapists, drug addicts, or murderers. The parents and teachers of such children often testify that they were literally "different from birth," or started showing signs of serious behavioral disturbance by the age of two or three—long before social or psychological factors could be blamed. Many others turned "feral" as the result of brain injuries, drug abuse, toxic exposure, or other physical insults.

In many other cases, brain dysfunction combines with social factors—gang pressures, poverty, broken homes—to push an at-risk individual over the edge. This is especially true now, when the social structures that once offered external controls, from churches and strict schools to close-knit families and neighborhoods, are crumbling. In the absence of *external* social controls, the biologically vulnerable child whose brain cannot create its own *internal* controls often is in serious trouble.

Of course, biology is only one piece of a very large puzzle. But the evidence I'll review in this book clearly indicates that much of the school failure, emotional turmoil, conduct problems, and irrational behavior we see in today's children is directly due to environmental hazards that compromise the integrity of their developing brains.

Why a wave of dyslogic now?

Skeptics may argue that our brains should be, in many ways, safer and healthier than in previous generations. And, to some degree, this is true. We have better sanitation and more advanced medical technology (including vaccines which, the medical community claims, improve our children's health). We have unlimited access to food, and starvation is almost unheard of in our country. We've taken some major steps to remove toxins from our environment, for instance by banning leaded gas and some pesticides such as DDT and chlordane. We know far more about what causes many diseases, and how to prevent them. All of this should translate into healthier bodies and, thus, healthier brains.

But for every step we take in the right direction, we take several in various wrong directions. As I'll explain in Part II, we actually are increasing, rather than decreasing, health hazards. Currently, industries use more than 1000 chemicals that have the potential to harm the brain.[2] Most of the estrogen-mimicking chemicals that we now use indiscriminately, and which pollute much of our drinking water, weren't even invented a few generations ago. Fertilizers and pesticides, now strongly linked to behavior and learning problems, are pumped into the environment in record amounts, and vast quantities of artificial additives are poured into our foods. And even the very harmful toxins we've started to control, such as lead and mercury and PCBs, will continue to pollute our environment for generations to come—if not forever.

Moreover, the diet that most children eat today is poor enough to cause widespread subclinical malnutrition. Such malnutrition often begins in infancy or in utero, when the brain is developing rapidly. In addition, large numbers of our children are exposed before birth to damaging chemicals from tobacco, drugs, and alcohol. During and after birth, nearly all are exposed to questionable medical treatments, from anesthesia and labor-inducing drugs during delivery, to massive dosing with antibiotics, to an ever-increasing list of vaccines that contain formaldehyde, aluminum, mercury, and other highly toxic substances, not to mention live viruses. "Given the enormous number of nutritional, environmental, and lifestyle threats currently facing the developing child," physician Joseph Beasley says, "it is little wonder that the number of children with learning and behavioral disorders is growing."[3]

The good news is that we have the science and the technology to identify the threats to our children's mental health. And while these threats are many, and some are ubiquitous, a large number of them can be controlled or even eliminated.

Can we fix a wounded brain?

The idea that dyslogical behavior stems from brain dysfunction frightens many people who believe that this means such problems are untreatable. This may be the main reason why we've turned to psychosocial interventions, which hold out the promise of fixing bad behavior simply by changing school curricula, or making parents nicer, or raising children's self-esteem.

But in reality, it is these psychosocial programs that have failed, and it is biological approaches that hold out the greatest promise for preventing and treating dyslogical behavior, academic failure, and even criminality. We can reduce children's exposure to dangerous toxins, and in many cases remove existing toxins from their bodies. We can prevent or correct malnourishment. We can reduce the incidence of prematurity, birth complications, head injuries, and drug-induced brain damage. We can diagnose and often treat certain medical disorders linked to criminal behavior. But we can do this only when we recognize that crime is not simply a social disease, but also a biologi- cal one.

Clearly, of course, we can't cure all biologically based dyslogic. In every generation, there are people whose brains are irreparably damaged by prenatal insults, accidents, disease, or other traumas. Many children's brains may be forever malformed, subtly or severely, because their mothers drank during pregnancy or their fathers beat them violently. Other children's brains will be permanently damaged by early malnutrition or severe genetic defects.

But for each of these people, there are many more whose brains have the potential to be strong and sane—or, if subjected to enough hazards, to be dyslogical or even insane. Often, we can save these children with amazingly simple and inexpensive interventions, such as the addition of half a milligram of folic acid to a mother's diet to help prevent neural tube defects, or the use of simple lead-screening tests to reveal lead toxicity while its effects can still be reversed. And even children with irreversible damage—for instance, those with fetal alcohol syndrome or genetic defects—frequently exhibit remarkable improvement when the environmental insults that add to their burden are corrected or when nutritional supplements improve brain function. I've seen autistic children recover, mentally retarded children make huge gains in IQ, depressed children blossom, and children considered to be severely emotionally disturbed become calm and loving, all with the help of the biological interventions I discuss in this book.

Addressing dyslogic on a national basis, rather than one child at a time, will of course require wide-scale and sometimes expensive solutions. We need to reduce the toxins in our air, water, and soil, and improve our food supply. In addition, we need to reevaluate potentially dangerous medical practices such as the excessive immunization of young infants, and we need to shift from the use of psychiatric drugs as a quick fix—the current practice of the medical community—to a focus on real diagnosis and appropriate treatment of brain dysfunction. But the cost of such interventions would be small, in comparison to their benefits—and their impact on the future of our nation.

A word about dyslogic and genes

Some people worry that any investigation into the biological roots of dyslogic will implicate genes, and that such findings will lead to the prejudgment or persecution of people who carry these genes. This argument, however, reflects an outdated view of genetics.

Modern research makes it clear that genes play a role in dyslogic, but also that there are no specific "dyslogic genes." Rather, there are myriad genes that can interact in complex ways with environmental hazards to increase the risk of brain dysfunction. When we understand these interactions, we can use our knowledge, not to persecute individuals whose genes put them at risk, but to optimize their environments to prevent problems before they occur.

A good example involves lead poisoning. Scientists are investigating variations in the ALAD (delta-aminolevulinic acid dehydratase) gene that appear to make certain children more susceptible to the damaging effects of lead toxicity, a major cause of dyslogical behavior.[4]

If we establish that specific variants of this gene indeed put certain children at higher risk for lead poisoning, we can screen for these variants. When we find children who possess them, we can caution health practitioners to monitor these children for even slightly elevated lead levels. We can take particularly aggressive steps to protect this group of children from excess lead exposure. We can recommend that children with this genetic vulnerability not drink water treated with silicofluorides, which can increase the uptake of lead (see Chapter 6). And we can take steps to improve the diets of these children, because high levels of vitamin C, calcium, and several other nutrients can help clear lead from the body.

For such children and millions of others with genetic vulnerabilities that make them targets for dyslogic, there is much to gain from increasing our knowledge about genetic influences on crime and other forms of dyslogical behavior, and much to lose if we are too timid to seek this knowledge. As Ann Moir and David Jessel ask in *A Mind to Crime*, "Are we so fearful that this knowledge could be abused that we dare not contemplate using it positively, creatively, and to society's—and the individual's—benefit?"[5]

While genes play a role in dyslogical behavior, and I devote several sections of this book to discussing their effects, scientific evidence strongly indicates that environmental threats, including toxins, diet deficiencies, and other man-made problems, may play a far larger role in making our children's brains malfunction. Where a child is blessed with a strong constitution and a good environment, such insults may merely make him or her somewhat less competent, or somewhat less moral. But for less fortunate children, environmental hazards can cause a lifetime of grief, trouble, and despair—a lifetime of dyslogic.

Are we in the midst of a nationwide epidemic of dyslogic—an epidemic that results not in cancer or heart disease, but in impaired brains that can't think well, can't exert control over behavior, and can't tell right from wrong? If so, we cannot combat this epidemic unless we understand its scope and causes. In the following chapters, I'll outline the evidence that large numbers of children are falling prey to "dyslogic syndrome." I'll describe the brain cripplers, from diet to toxins to misguided medical interventions, that place our children at risk for devastating brain dysfunction. Most important, I will describe what you can do—as a parent, a teacher, a medical professional, a judge, or even just a concerned citizen—to help stop this epidemic.

Notes

1   Macko, S. (1996) "Kids with no hope, no fear, no rules, and no life expectancy." Emergency Net News, 18 May. Available at www.emergency.com/juvycrim.htm (accessed 4 October 2007).

2   Grandjean, P. and Landrigan, P. (2006) "Developmental neurotoxicity of industrial chemicals." *The Lancet 368*, 9553, 2167–78.

3   Beasley, J. (1991) *The Betrayal of Health*. New York: Times Books.

4   Smith, C.M., Wang, X., Hu, H. and Kelsey, K.T. (1995) "A polymorphism in the delta-aminolevulinic acid dehydratase gene may modify the pharmacokinetics and toxicity of lead." *Environmental Health Perspectives 103*, 3, 248–53. See also: Hu, H., Wu, M.T., Cheng, Y., Sparrow, D., Weiss, S. and Kelsey, K. (2001) "The delta-aminolevulinic acid dehydratase (ALAD) polymorphism and bone and blood lead levels in community-exposed men: The Normative Aging Study." *Environmental Health Perspectives 109*, 8, 827–32.

5   Moir, A. and Jessel, D. (1997) *A Mind to Crime*. London: Signet, p.143.

CHAPTER 2

The Dyslogic Epidemic's Victims: America's "Mad," "Bad," and "Dumbed Down" Children

"In our office we have asked [teachers] if they have observed a change in children during their teaching careers. Without exception, they have replied there has been a dramatic change, most notably since the 1970s. Steadily increasing numbers of children, they report, are restless, impulsive, less focused, less able to maintain sustained concentration, and therefore, less able to learn."

—Harold Buttram, M.D., and Richard Piccola, M.H.A., in *Our Toxic World: Who is Looking After our Kids?*, 1997

In the late 1970s, I worked as a senior research psychologist for the United States Navy. During this time, the Navy asked me to investigate an unexpected problem: many of the Navy's new recruits lacked even the basic skills needed by young sailors.

Increasingly, these recruits couldn't read at an elementary school level. They couldn't do even low-level math problems. They couldn't learn quickly in the classroom, or solve problems efficiently in the field. They couldn't understand the training manuals that previous generations of sailors had mastered easily. They were poor at following orders, "sassed" their instructors, and got into fights with the other recruits.

Moreover, incidents of deviant and criminal behavior were escalating among new sailors. More recruits were committing rapes or other crimes, going AWOL, and receiving dishonorable discharges.

The first question I addressed was a simple one: *Is this problem real?*

It was a necessary question, because many factors, such as a change in the procedures for reporting problems, could lead to the misperception that a problem existed. Thus, I didn't know if I was looking at an artifact—the appearance of a problem, where none really existed—or at a real and serious change, not just in the Navy's recruits, but perhaps in the population in general.

With the help of my assistant Gerald Larson, I conducted an in-depth investigation of many different variables. In the end, the over-whelming data, compiled into a paper called "The Manpower Quality Decline,"[1] forced us to come to the conclusion we did not like. We found that the decline in Navy recruits—both in "brain power" and in behavior—was indeed very real. More disturbing, we found that this decline mirrored a dramatic decline in the civilian world: falling test scores, a drop in student performance, and increasing crime and patho-logical behavior.

At the time, some people accused us of being alarmists. Since that time, however, newer studies continue to reveal evidence that, since the 1940s and 1950s, something mysterious and troubling has affected our younger generation's ability to think, learn, and behave, as well as their physical health.

More early signs of this crisis came to light in 1983, when Dr. Peter Budetti reported that physical and mental defects in newborns had *doubled* since the mid-1900s. Since the 1950s, Budetti said, the percentage of babies with a physical, mental, or learning defect severe enough to be detectable at birth had risen from 2 to 4 percent.[2] The findings startled doctors because, as physician Barbara Stanfield noted, "the 1950s were a terrible time for children because of polio and other diseases... [With] improvements in medical care one might expect real improvements, not the other way around."[3]

Nearly two decades later, in 1999, researchers at Johns Hopkins University reported that rates of mental and physical birth defects were still rising steadily.[4] A study in 2002 reported that one in every 12 American children and teens—8 percent, or *double* the number that alarmed Budetti in 1983—suffers from a physical or mental disability.[5]

We aren't merely talking about minor disabilities, either. New figures indicate that the rate of severe and persistent mental illnesses (including schizophrenia, bipolar disorder, severe depression, panic disorder, and obsessive-compulsive disorder) rose from approximately 4 per 1000 in 1958 to as high as 19 per 1000 today. Says psychiatrist E. Fuller Torrey:

> We are [faced] with an epidemic of schizophrenia and bipolar disorder that presently affects 4 million Americans, four times more than are infected with HIV… An epidemic that is so insidious…that it is barely noticed, an invisible plague. An epidemic that increased as much as 10-fold over the last century and that appears to still be increasing.[6]

The prevalence of childhood autism also has risen from 1 in 2500 to as many as 1 in 166, and childhood depression, once almost unheard of, now affects as many as one in eight adolescents and one in thirty-three children.[7] Commenting on the rates of mental illness in children, Joseph Woolston, M.D., Chief of Child Psychiatry at Yale-New Haven Hospital, said in 2002, "If this were an infectious disease, we would call this an epidemic."[8]

As we entered the new millennium, a Boston physician's organization issued a frightening report detailing the evidence of what they termed "an epidemic of developmental, learning, and behavioral disabilities" among children. The report estimated that nearly 12 million children suffer from one or more of these problems, which "have widespread societal implications, from health and education costs to the repercussions of criminal behavior."[9] Their fears were echoed by researcher Julie Magno Zito and colleagues, who reported in 2000 that approximately 150,000 U.S. preschoolers were taking psychotropic drugs, including antidepressants, Ritalin, and antipsychotics.[10]

These studies show that all is not well with America's younger generations, and the real-life evidence is all around us. The signs of widespread dyslogic which first became obvious in the 1960s and 1970s are now all too clear. Children barely in their teens are committing rapes, murders, and other brutal crimes, a phenomenon almost unknown in the 1940s and 1950s. We see academic deficits even among many of our best students, a "dumbing down" of our culture, and a workforce growing less competent and less literate than ever before. Rates of depression and bipolar disorder, conditions once almost unheard of in children, are skyrocketing. At the same time, enrollment in our special education classes is mushrooming, and millions of children line up in school nurses' offices at lunchtime each day in our schools to take major psychoactive drugs.

> *Reporter Joan Lowy recently interviewed Dr. Martha Herbert, a pediatric neurologist at Massachusetts General Hospital who treats children with behavior disorders. Talking about how she'd recently treated a four-year-old who'd tried to kill a sibling, Herbert commented, "I've had several cases like that. It's scary because this kind of thing hardly ever used to happen."* [11]

Unfortunately, it's easier to ignore an epidemic of subtle brain disabilities, particularly when they affect something as hard to measure as mental functioning, than it is to ignore an epidemic of diseases that are clearly physical. Doctors are currently raising a hue and cry about dramatic increases in childhood asthma, brain cancer, and diabetes—increases that are not surprising, because what harms behavior often harms the body in other ways—but the public is largely unaware of the concurrent rise in equally crippling learning and behavioral problems. Yet the evidence of a "mental meltdown" is all around us, in the form of millions of children who are failing at life and handicapping all of society in the process. In this chapter, I'll look at three groups of these children:

- The thousands of young predators who rape and rob and kill without reason, mercy, or any apparent awareness of the consequences of their actions.

- The millions of learning disabled and mentally disordered children currently overwhelming our special education and mental health systems.

- The tens of millions of seemingly "normal" children who are having difficulty mastering even drastically scaled-down schoolwork and the most basic rules of civilized life.

Destructive dyslogic: the criminals

As I write this, crowds of chattering children are passing by my window on their way to school. It's a cheerful and innocent scene, straight out of a Norman Rockwell painting.

The news reports in my daily paper, however, reveal a darker image. Today, CNN is reporting that a SWAT team in Florida shot a 15-year-old middle school student after the boy pulled out a gun in class and then threatened SWAT agents with it. A few months ago, a high school student in Tennessee shot and killed an assistant principal. Earlier the same year, a student at Red Lake High School in Minnesota gunned down his grandparents and then drove to school, where he murdered seven students and staff members before killing himself.

What is most disturbing to me and my colleagues in the field of psychology is the senseless nature of these and many other crimes committed by today's children. When I was growing up, my parents might worry about having our car stolen, or about being mugged for our money. They never worried, however, that their children would be shot to death by a student in the school cafeteria. It never occurred to us that our friends might knife us in an argument over a game, or beat us to death if we tossed an insult at them. Until recent decades, young criminals typically stole cars for joyrides, or shoplifted beer from the local store—not smart crimes, but easy enough to understand. Today, they're likely to set their sisters on fire, or beat old women to death, often "just for the thrill of it."

In addition to exhibiting unprecedented savagery, today's young criminals often wound or kill with no idea of the consequences, either to themselves or to their victims. One 17-year-old, for instance, shot his mother in the kitchen with a shotgun, after watching the movie *American Beauty*, because of its transcendent portrayal of death. Afterward he told a teacher, "I *love* my mother. If you saw what I did, you'd understand."[12] Another young criminal wondered why people didn't feel sorry for him, because he missed the friend he'd shot to death. Eric Harris and Dylan Klebold, who killed 12 students and a teacher at Columbine High School before shooting themselves to death, said in a video made before the crime that the purpose of the murders was to "kickstart a revolution." And a 14-year-old who participated in the fatal gang beating of a man in

Milwaukee told police he "felt kind of bad," because he didn't realize that 20 kids hitting a man with fists, shovels, tree limbs, and chairs could actually kill him.[13]

Tragic dyslogic: the learning disabled, mentally disabled, and "living disabled"

Children who shoot their classmates or rape their sisters capture our attention with their horrifying acts. At the same time, however, the dyslogic epidemic is claiming millions of quieter victims: children suffering from hyperactivity, learning disabilities, and mental disorders that make their lives a constant, and all too often unsuccessful, struggle against failure. While these children's dyslogic is less visible than that of a young murderer or rapist, their suffering—and the costs that we as a society pay for their dyslogic—are enormous.

The number of these hyperactive and learning disabled children is growing at a rate that almost surpasses belief. According to a poll taken in 2003, one in three American families has coped with a child with a learning disability or a mental illness. "These are staggering numbers," said Shelly Hearne, who is the executive director of Trust for America's Health. "The implication is that we have a significant problem out there that, we are not adequately addressing."[14]

While some of this increase may stem from better diagnosis, all of the doctors I talk with agree that they now see far, far more children with hyperactivity, dyslexia, and other learning problems than they saw even ten years ago. One group of learning disabilities experts reported that, between the mid-seventies and the mid-nineties, the number of learning disabled children served by schools increased by 198 percent. "Were these epidemic-like figures interpreted by the Centers for Disease Control," they said, "one might reasonably expect to find a quarantine imposed on the public schools of America."[15]

Why are children with hyperactivity and learning disorders included in a book about dyslogical behavior? Because children with these disorders are at exceedingly high risk of committing illogical, violent, destructive, or harmful acts—in short, of being "dyslogical." The results, on a personal and societal level, are catastrophic.

Professionals tend to treat hyperactivity solely as a behavioral problem, and learning disabilities solely as an academic problem. In doing so, they fail to acknowledge the most crippling symptom of many children with hyperactivity or learning disabilities: their inability to think logically, and, thus, to behave logically.

A number of children *do* have isolated problems with attention, spelling, reading, or math, and can learn to compensate for these deficits and succeed in life. But school problems are just the tip of the iceberg for millions of other children labeled as hyperactive or learning disabled; what many of these children really suffer from is not just a learning problem but a *thinking* problem, a problem often so serious and so pervasive that it affects all aspects of their lives. And with rates of learning disabilities going through the ceiling, the dyslogical behavior manifested by these children is increasingly affecting our entire society.

While only 5 to 10 percent of the population is learning disabled, up to three-fourths of delinquents suffer from learning disabilities[16] and as many as half of prison inmates have dyslexia.[17] Robert Thatcher and Diana Fishbein, who have studied brain wave patterns in learning disabled criminals, aren't surprised by such findings. They say, "Many delinquents have learning disorders... Their thinking is cloudy and unsophisticated. They can't read or write. If they're antisocial, they have difficulty telling right from wrong; they can't properly evaluate consequences. Eventually, this can lead to criminality."[18]

In his seminal 1975 paper, "The Dyslogic Syndrome,"[19] John Wacker identified a cluster of cognitive and behavioral symptoms seen in many hyperactive and learning disabled children. They include:

- failures in judgment
- an inability to understand the consequences of their actions
- selfish or narcissistic behavior
- impulsivity
- an inability to postpone immediate gratification in pursuit of long-term goals
- short attention span

- "catastrophic" reactions to minor upsets

- deficits in abstract thinking

- poor social skills and, often, poor eye contact with others

- shallow emotional relationships, and an inability to form positive friendships

- lack of empathy toward people or animals

- an excessive need for excitement

- an inability to learn from experience

- low frustration levels, and a lack of inhibition.

Translated into real life, this means that millions of children with learning disabilities are at extreme risk of committing acts that will cause harm to themselves or others. Because they have little regard for the consequences of their acts, dyslogical hyperactive or learning disabled individuals are candidates for criminal behavior, alcoholism, and drug abuse. They are tempted by both the immediate gratification of a drug "high," and the acceptance they find among the drug crowd. Learning disabled adolescents and adults also are much more likely than their peers to engage in promiscuous and unsafe sex, and to become pregnant or to father children during their teens.

Overall, the outlook for dyslogical learning disabled or hyperactive adults, both socially and vocationally, is dismal. One study of adults diagnosed in childhood as hyperactive reported that, compared to controls, the attention deficit hyperactivity disorder (ADHD) subjects "complete less schooling, hold lower-ranking occupations, and continue to suffer from poor self-esteem and social skills deficits. In addition, significantly more [ADHD subjects] than controls exhibit an antisocial personality."[20] Another study found that childhood hyperactivity, even when not combined with conduct problems, strongly predicted later violence, social problems, academic underachievement, and defiant and disruptive behaviors.[21] And a third, more recent study of adults with ADHD, most of them diagnosed in childhood, found that they were twice as likely as other adults to have arrest records, and nearly three times as likely to be unemployed at the time of the study.[22]

Clearly, the massive rise we're seeing in the numbers of children diagnosed as learning disabled has serious consequences for society, because that number translates into millions of lives in jeopardy—both those of dyslogical learning disabled children and those of the "bystanders" whom their dyslogical behavior affects. But an even more frightening affliction—mental illness—also is stalking our children, and claiming millions of victims.

Childhood's new demons: depression and manic depression

Just as rates of learning disabilities are soaring, so are rates of depression and bipolar disease (also known as manic depressive illness). Like learning disabled children, children identified as depressed or manic depressive are at high risk of failure and of suicide. They are also at high risk for committing violent acts against others, as evidenced by the high percentage of school shooters who were taking antidepressants at the times of their attacks (see Chapter 4).

Like learning disabilities, depression and manic depressive illness are "dyslogical" disorders, which cloud their sufferers' thinking and make it impossible for them to plan for the future rationally and interpret events logically. In the manic phase of bipolar disorder in particular, children and teens can commit irrational or even deadly acts.

As with hyperactivity and learning disabilities, the rates of depression and bipolar disorder appear to be soaring. While depression in children was almost unheard of a few decades ago, around 20 percent of today's young people will have one or more episodes of major depression by the time they reach adulthood.[23] In addition, depression is striking children at younger ages than in past decades.[24]

With millions of children diagnosed as hyperactive or attention-disordered, millions more suffering from a diagnosed learning disability, and nearly a million children and teenagers diagnosed as depressed, it's imperative that we find out what is changing in our world, and how it is affecting these troubled children's brains. Moreover, what we learn may affect not just these children, but all of us. The learning disabled and mentally disabled children whose numbers are increasing so rapidly may be, in effect, our "mine canaries": people who, because of biological vulnerability, are among the first to fall victim to an epidemic which will eventually affect millions more of our children—and generations to come. And, in fact, there are disturbing signs that the epidemic is striking not only those we consider troubled or disabled, but those we consider normal as well.

Hidden dyslogic: when "normal" isn't

When educator Jane Healy interviewed teachers for her 1990 book, *Endangered Minds*,[25] she heard the same pattern of comments at every school: "Every year I seem to 'water down' the material even more," "I use with gifted sixth graders a lot of what I did with average fifth graders in '65–'66," "Ten years ago I gave students materials and they were able to figure out the experiment. Now I have to walk them through the activities step by step."

Healy wrote about the frustration of teachers who must continually "dumb down" their curricula to match the declining abilities of students—even the gifted ones. When she surveyed 300 teachers, she said:

> I was amazed by the unanimity of response. Yes, attention spans are noticeably shorter. Yes, reading, writing, and oral language skills seem to be declining—even in the 'best' neighborhoods. Yes, no matter how 'bright,' students are less able to bend their minds around difficult problems in math, science, and other subjects.

In spite of continuing educational reforms, things haven't changed much for the better since Healy wrote her book. In 1999, for example, New York City tested its students and found that 77 percent of them couldn't do math well and 65 percent flunked language arts. "God, what a mess," one New York parent commented. "If they can't read and can't do math, what can our kids do, besides watch TV?"[26]

Similarly, the U.S. Department of Education reported in August 2001 that more than one-third of high school seniors do not have even a basic competence in mathematics. "This means," a report in *Scientific American* notes, "that they don't understand elementary algebra, have little conception of probability and can't make simple measurements of the kind required of a beginning carpenter."[27]

Children's test scores are creeping up in the wake of the "No Child Left Behind" education reforms, but they're still anemic. And older kids aren't doing any better; in 2006, the National Survey of America's College Students found that only 40 percent of college seniors can handle basic skills such as telling the difference between fact and commentary in a newspaper editorial, reading maps and instruction manuals accurately, or calculating a waiter's tip correctly.[28]

A related problem cited by overwhelming numbers of teachers is the short attention span of today's students, many of whom can't pay attention long enough to make sense of a lecture, book, or play. This subclinical attention deficit disorder is becoming painfully obvious in society as a whole, and particularly among teens and young adults. Television programs and magazines are responding to this trend by continually "dumbing down" their content; a comparison of newspaper and magazine content in the 1950s and in current issues, for instance, reveals a dramatic decline in the length of articles and the seriousness of their topics, and a corresponding increase in "puff" news and photos of celebrities.

There is one seemingly bright spot that stands out in all this gloom: on IQ tests, scores are rising. American children given older IQ tests from the 1930s and 1940s score higher on them than did children in those earlier decades. According to tests, in fact, the average IQ of American children is rising by about 15 points every 50 years. But the increase appears to reflect not higher intelligence, but rather greater access to education since the 1930s, and the effects of universal exposure to the media. Dr. James Flynn, who identified the IQ trend now named after him ("the Flynn Effect"), speculates that IQ test scores measure not intelligence, but instead a specialized type of problem-solving that may not be applicable in the real world.[29]

While the validity of test results can be debated, the concrete evidence of a dyslogic epidemic among "normal" students is all too clear. Across the country, graduation requirements have dropped, colleges and universities have lowered entrance requirements, and there is a sharp increase in the number of remedial courses on college campuses. College students today are doing high school level work in reading, math, and science, and are struggling to comprehend it. When high school students nearing graduation were tested in the early 1990s to determine their aptitude for analytic writing—the ability to provide evidence, reason logically, and make a well-developed point—only *four-tenths of 1 percent* of them performed at a level that would have been considered adequate for college freshmen a few decades earlier.[30] This is a crucial finding, because it dispels the myth that declining college performance is due solely to the fact that colleges are now open to increasing numbers of disadvantaged students. This fact, while true, cannot explain less than half of 1 percent of students performing at levels considered normal only 20 years before!

Each year millions of dumbed down students leave school and enter the workforce, with predictable results. In 1999, an American Management Association study found that more than 38 percent of job applicants taking basic skills tests lacked basic competence in reading, writing, or math and were virtually unemployable except in entry-level jobs.[31] In 2004, a survey of manufacturers found that more than half of the firms had difficulty finding qualified workers. Said one manufacturer, "They can't even express themselves in a simple sentence."[32] More evidence of trouble comes from the military, which recently reported that one-third of military recruits have arrest records, and that one-fourth of Army career enlisted personnel commit criminal acts while on active duty.[33]

The morality crisis

The dyslogic epidemic is profoundly changing our schools and our workplaces, but the effects of the epidemic are seen everywhere—not just in the classroom or the office. Many children and adults are having increasing difficulty not just with reading, writing, and arithmetic, but with behaviors and skills that aren't part of a school curriculum: responsibility, self-control, judgment, and empathy.

As a result, we are seeing an escalating breakdown of societal rules. A nationwide survey of teens by the Josephson Institute of Ethics in 2006 found that, over the previous year, nearly two-thirds cheated on exams, 23 percent stole from a parent or other relative, 19 percent stole from a friend, and 28 percent shoplifted.[34] Worse, increasing numbers of students are threatening teachers with guns, knives, and fists. Foul language and disobedience, once almost unknown in schools, are commonplace, and a third of America's teachers have considered quitting because of the breakdown in discipline.[35]

What's even more startling is that these problems are common even in young children. A friend of mine, who teaches kindergarten, reports that she routinely has to restrain children who attempt to bite, hit, and kick her—behaviors virtually never seen in a kindergarten classroom in the 1950s or 1960s. Ronald Stephens, executive director of the National School Safety Center, says, "Teachers, more and more, are becoming targets of violence from students at younger and younger ages."[36]

Interestingly, however, the problems we're seeing aren't limited to the U.S., or even the Western hemisphere. Even the Japanese, famous for classroom discipline and high academic expectations, are reporting signs of societal breakdown: beginning in the 1990s, Japanese newspapers reported a dramatic increase in fatal shootings, and more recently Japanese educators expressed alarm about a terrifying new trend of entire classrooms of children going berserk—a phenomenon they call "classroom collapse."[37,38] Clearly, whatever is happening isn't just "our problem"—it's everyone's.

A central point of this book is that the problem behaviors we see in our children are, to a great degree, evidence of a biological epidemic of brain dysfunction. What effect would such an epidemic have? First, we'd see a dramatic upswing in the number of people diagnosed as hyperactive, learning disabled, depressed, or attention-disordered. Given the strong link between criminality and brain dysfunction, we'd also see many senseless criminal acts being committed by adults, teens, and even children. And we'd see signs of subclinical brain dysfunction in the population as a whole, with significant numbers of supposedly normal individuals doing poorly in school and on the job, and having difficulty following rules, acting decently, and controlling their behavior. This is, as I've outlined, exactly what we're seeing, and it is a trend that has profound and frightening implications for our society.

The millions of dollars America currently spends in an attempt to reverse this trend through school reforms and juvenile mental health programs demonstrates that we recognize, at least to some degree, that many of our children are in trouble. Unfortunately, as I'll show in the next chapter, these measures aren't making a measurable dent in our epidemic of dyslogic. If an invisible and sinister foe is impairing the brains of millions of children, we need to identify this foe and conquer it—but before we can, we need to analyze our current efforts to address our epidemic of dyslogical and dangerous behavior, and understand why these efforts are failing so miserably.

Notes

1   Rimland, B. and Larson, G. (1981) "The Manpower quality decline: An ecological perspective." *Armed Forces and Society*, Fall.

2   Cited by Lyons, R. in "Physical and mental disabilities in newborns doubled in 25 years," *New York Times*, July 18, 1983.

3   Ibid.

4   "Birth defects rising in the U.S.," *Reuters*, November 18, 1999.

5   Cohn, D. (2002) "Number of young handicapped Americans growing." *Star-Telegram*, July 6.

6   Torrey, E.F. (2002) "Severe psychiatric disorders may be increasing." *Psychiatric Times 19*, 4. Available at http://psychiatrictimes.com/showArticle.jhtml?articleID=175801711 (accessed 26 September 2007).

7   National Alliance for the Mentally Ill, factsheet, "Early onset depression," 2002. Available at www.nami.org/helpline/depression-child.html (accessed 10 october 2007).

8   Cited on the website of "The Campaign for American Academy of Child and Adolescent Psychiatry. Available at www.campaignforamericaskids.org/ 6A_mental_health.html.

9   Greater Boston Physicians for Social Responsibility (2000) "In harm's way— toxic threats to child development." Available at http://psr.igc.org/ ihw-project.htm (accessed 10 October 2007).

10 Zito, J.M., Safer, D.J., dosReis, S., Gardner, J.F., Boles, M. and Lynch, F. "Trends in the prescribing of psychotropic medications to preschoolers." *Journal of the American Medical Association 283*, 1025–30. Cited in: Allen, A. "From diapers to drugs." *Salon.com*, February 23, 2000.

11 Lowy, J. (2003) "Canaries in the mine—evidence of chemical effects on kids mounts." *Scripps Howard News Service*, December 20.

12 Powers, R. (2002) "The apocalypse of adolescence." *Atlantic Monthly*, March.

13 McBee, T. (2002) "At liberty: Little monsters." *Arkansas Democrat-Gazette*, October 8.

14 Lowy, J. (2003) "Poll: 30 percent of families have children with learning disorders." *Scripps Howard News Service*, December 16.

15 MacMillan, D.L. *et al.* cited in "Learning disabilities as operationally defined by schools," D.L. MacMillan and Gary N. Siperstein, paper presented at the Learning Disabilities Summit, Washington, DC 2001.

16 Larson, K.A. (1988) "A research review and alternative hypothesis explaining the link between learning disability and delinquency." *Journal of Learning Disabilities 21*, 6, 357–63.

17 Moody, K.C., Holzer, C.E., Roman, M.J., Paulsen, K.A., Freeman, D.H., Haynes, M. and James, T.N. (2000) "Prevalence of dyslexia among Texas prison inmates." *Journal of Texas Medicine 96*, 6, 69–75; Jensen, J., Lindgren, M., Meurling, A.W., Ingvar, D.H. and Levander, S. (1999) "Dyslexia among Swedish prison inmates in relation to neuropsychology and personality." *Journal of the International Neuropsychological Society 5*, 5, 452–61; and Santiago, H.C. (1995) "Visual and educational dysfunctions in a group of Hispanic residents of a juvenile detention center." Presentation to the American Academy of Optometry.

18 Fishbein, D.H. and Thatcher, R.W. "Nutritional and electrophysiological indices of maladaptive behavior." Paper presented at the MIT Conference on Research Strategies for Assessing the Behavioral Effects and Nutrients, Cambridge, MA, 1982.

19 Wacker, J. (1975) "The Dyslogic Syndrome." Presentation at the conference, Learning Disabilities: The Interface Between Brain-based Dysfunctions and Adult Psychiatric Disturbances, sponsored by the Menninger Foundation and the Association for Children and Adults with Learning Disabilities, Topeka, Kansas, November 22–23.

20 Mannuzza, S. and Klein, R.G. (2000) "Long-term prognosis in attention-deficit/hyperactivity disorder." *Child and Adolescent Psychiatric Clinics of North America 9*, 3, 711–26.

21 Taylor, E., Chadwick, O., Heptinstall, E. and Danckaerts, M. (1996) "Hyperactivity and conduct problems as risk factors for adolescent development." *Journal of the American Academy of Child and Adolescent Psychiatry 35*, 9, 1213–26.

22 Biederman, J., Faraone, S., Spencer, T., Mick, E., Monuteaux, M. and Aleardi, M. (2006) "Functional impairments in adults with self-reports of diagnosed ADHD." *Journal of Clinical Psychiatry 67*, 4, 524–40.

23 Fact sheet, National Depression Screening Day, 2006.

24 "Depression in children and adolescents." Fact sheet, National Institute of Mental Health, August 2000.

25 Healy, J.M. (1990) *Endangered Minds.* New York: Touchstone/Simon & Schuster.

26 Shin, P.H.B. and Gendar, A. (1999) "77% flunk new 8th grade state exam." *New York Daily News*, November 6.

27 Doyle, R. (2001) "Can't read, can't count." *Scientific American*, October.

28 "Declining literacy skills: Another analysis highlights a massive problem," *Las Vegas Review-Journal*, March 2, 2006.

29 Healy, J.M. (1990) *Endangered Minds*. New York: Touchstone/Simon & Schuster.

30 Singal, D. (1991) "The other crisis in American education." *The Atlantic 268*, November, 5, 59–74.

31 Doyle, R. (2001) "Can't read, can't count." *Scientific American*, October.

32 Hagenbaugh, B. (2004) "Good help hard to find for manufacturers." *USA Today*, April 16.

33 Silverstein, K. (2004) "Pentagon alerted to trouble in ranks." *Los Angeles Times*, July 1.

34 "Biennial report card: The ethics of American youth," Josephson Institute of Ethics, 2006.

35 "Why schools are failing," *Parade*, August 1, 2004.

36 Cited in Wallis, C. (2003) "Does kindergarten need cops?" Times Magazine, 7 December. Available at www.time.com/time/magazine/article/0,9171,1101031215-556865,00.html (accessed 25 September 2007).

37 "Japan fears becoming a 'gun society' like U.S.; shooting cases dramatically up," AP wire service report, *Arizona Republic*, December 26, 1994.

38 French, H. (2002) "Educators try to tame Japan's blackboard jungles." *New York Times*, September 23.

CHAPTER 3

Why "Nurture" Fixes
Can't Cure Dyslogic

"Blame my parents."

—Popular t-shirt slogan

When a child "goes bad," we typically place the blame on an unhealthy psychological environment. We blame troubled children on poor schools, TV, video games, and violent movies. We blame poverty for poor children's failures, and, ironically, we blame a culture of excess for wealthy children's aberrant behavior. But most of all, we blame parents. They "should have known" that their kids were troubled. They "should have done something." They were too strict, too lenient, too controlling, too negligent, too mean. They should have lived in better neighborhoods, put their kids in better schools, cuddled them more, or spoiled them less.

As a result, we often attempt to fix dyslogical children by fixing their families through psychotherapy or counseling, on the assumption that dyslogic stems solely from a "nurture" defect. It's a seductive idea, but there's one big problem: the evidence doesn't support it. In reality, parents play a surprisingly small role in their children's mental health—and the upshot is that we're spending enormous amounts of time and money on psychological and sociological interventions that aren't doing any good.

Imagine a perfect mother and father who buy all the right toys, say all the right words, use the perfect disciplinary measures, and provide just the right amount of stimulation for their children. Now, picture the children of these wonderful parents. Wouldn't they be just perfect?

Not necessarily. In fact, they might not even be any better than average.

The late Dr. Benjamin Spock, America's most famous "baby doctor," conducted one of the earliest and most ambitious tests of the effects of family influence on children's success. In the 1950s, Spock arranged to provide intensive counseling for 21 families, so that these enlightened mothers and fathers could avoid the parenting mistakes that he blamed for children's later failures in life.

The best therapists Spock could find, including some trained by Sigmund Freud's daughter Anna, counseled these test families, teaching them how to interact lovingly and intelligently with their children. After this intensive therapy and training program ended, Spock followed the children for 13 years, expecting to see a dramatic difference between them and a control group of children whose parents had no therapy at all.

Much to his chagrin, however, Spock found that the children of the "super parents" were no more well adjusted than any other children. Spock himself admitted that, when it came to guessing which children would turn out well, "our predictors were no damn good." [1]

Obviously, there is some truth to the idea that an unpleasant or unstable environment affects a child. Abusive or grossly over-indulgent parents, bad schools, poverty, broken families, and exposure to violence *do* negatively influence the lives of many children. But can social factors explain a significant part of the symptoms of our dyslogic epidemic, from school shootings to a drop in academic performance to an escalating number of children diagnosed as learning disabled, depressed, attention-disordered, or hyperactive? Indeed, can social factors really account for *any one* of these problems, or—more to the point—solve any of them?

The answer, regardless of what psychological experts say, is no. Contrary to popular belief, years of research clearly reveal that there is little truth to the three almost-sacred yet fallacious psycho-sociological myths on which we've based our efforts to prevent or reverse dyslogical behavior.

Those fallacious but almost universally accepted beliefs are outlined below.

MYTH #1: MOST DEVIANCE STEMS FROM A BAD ENVIRONMENT, AND, IN PARTICULAR, FROM ABUSIVE OR NEGLECTFUL PARENTING

It surprises many people to learn that a large percentage of our most hardened criminals come from good and loving families. That's because the notion that bad parents cause troubled children has been solidly ingrained in Western culture since the days of Freud. One child advocacy group, for instance, says that adult delinquency and aggression may stem from "discipline described as lax or neglectful, as erratic or inconsistent, and as overly harsh or punitive"[2] (terms that could probably, in one way or another, describe any typical parent's disciplinary activities, at least on occasion).

In reality, however, one of the best kept secrets of the century is that *parents aren't very influential*, except in a genetic sense. Remarkably, research finds they have surprisingly little control, good or bad, over their children's emotional, behavioral, or social development. Furthermore, scientific studies reveal that different parenting techniques have almost no discernible effect on the outcome of children. Robert Hare, a leading authority on psychopathic behavior, has studied hundreds of remorseless killers and criminals and concludes, "We do not know why people become psychopaths, but current evidence leads us away from the commonly held idea that the behavior of parents bears sole or even primary responsibility for the disorder."[3] Another expert, David Rowe, says, "I seriously doubt that good child-rearing practices can greatly reduce an undesirable trait's prevalence, whether it be low IQ, criminality, or any other trait of social concern."[4]

Surprised? So was I, when I began to research this heretical idea. This was back in the 1950s, when Freudian theory still prevailed and experts blamed everything from bed-wetting to serial killing on bad mothers and fathers. Like most psychologists, I accepted this idea as gospel, and taught it to my students as gospel as well—until I started looking at the literature. Amazingly, I found, study after study reported exactly the opposite of what I'd been led to believe and what I was teaching. Parents, it seemed, weren't at all influential; they weren't able to create perfect children or, conversely, damage children permanently with a cross word or a spanking. In fact, research showed, they had little or no control over how their children turned out.

My revelation began with a single paper. Of the many millions of words that I have read during my lifetime, few, if any, have had a greater impact on me than an article published in 1957 by psychiatrist Ian Stevenson.[5] In it, he said, "If the experiences of childhood importantly influence the later personality, we should expect to find some correlation between such experiences and the later occurrence of mental disorders. In fact, no such correlations have ever been shown." I came across this article when starting the research that culminated in my book, *Infantile Autism*. At the time, I wanted to know on what basis psychiatrists and psychologists had concluded that autism was caused by bad mothering, a "fact" stated unequivocally by virtually every textbook in my field.

When I read Stevenson's quote, I was stunned. It directly contradicted what I had repeatedly been taught as absolute truth, and what I had subsequently taught to hundreds of college students. Starting with the references Stevenson cited, I spent months reading everything I could find. Amazingly, Stevenson was right! Among the myth-defying research findings that he and later researchers reported:

- Curious about what type of upbringing created successful children, Irving Stout and Grace Langdon studied more than a hundred children and young teens selected because they were very well adjusted. These students were happy, well liked and respected by other students, and able to control their emotions and think for themselves.

When the researchers evaluated these children's parents, Martin L. Gross reported in *The Psychological Society*, they found that "the answers were disappointing to psychological fans... The children were products of a diverse set of child-raising ideas, with no agreement by their parents as to what was correct in child rearing. Some came from poor homes, others from wealthy backgrounds. There were children who had one dead parent. Some of the parents had only been to grade school; others had college degrees. There was no special birth order, nor did only children predominate." More importantly, they reported, parenting techniques ranged from very strict and authoritarian to very lenient: "In some homes," they noted, "the parents spanked the children or even sent them to bed with only bread and milk for supper when they were 'bad.' In other homes, they used the modern 'Let's talk it over' technique." These different parenting styles had no effect whatsoever on the children's mental and emotional health.[6]

- Jean Macfarlane and colleagues followed approximately 200 people from childhood through adulthood, to see if (as expected) the people with tough childhoods would have problems as adults. They found, instead, that children from troubled homes often turned out to be very successful later on, while those who had many advantages—especially very popular children—often had trouble as adults.[7]

- After World War II, the Air Force, hoping to discover why certain officers, identified as highly superior, excelled both on the job and in their personal lives, asked the University of California's Berkeley Counseling Center to study the issue. The researchers conducting the study expected, of course, to find that these outstanding officers all came from stable, loving families, and had suffered little or no childhood trauma. They were astounded to find, on the contrary, that the 100 exceptional officers they studied came from family settings with as much "clinical pathology" as those of their ordinary psychiatric patients.[8]

If there's little reason to credit parents when their children do well, there is equally little reason to blame parents when their children go wrong. One study of 38 murderers found that 26 of them grew up in good and loving families, with no abuse or neglect that could explain their crimes.[9] And Robert Hare and colleagues found that, while *non*-psychopathic criminals were affected to a limited degree by their family backgrounds, "the quality of family life had absolutely no effect on the emergence of criminality in psychopaths…even a good family life that promotes healthy behavior in their siblings does little to deter psychopaths from their lives of callous self-gratification."[10]

The same appears true for more minor behaviors. Recently, researchers questioned nearly 500 teenage girls about how supportive and "in charge" their parents were. They also tallied up the girls' behavior problems, such as lying, stealing, or running away. The researchers found little evidence that parenting style affected the girls' behavior. (In fact, they found the opposite: parenting styles typically were a *response to*, rather than a *cause of*, the girls' problems.)[11]

The message is clear: children aren't permanently warped by parents who are too lenient or too strict, parents who work, parents who divorce, or parents who fail to show up at their Little League games—and more often than not, they aren't even warped permanently by parents with what professionals call "clinical pathology."

Likewise, the best parents, providing the best environments, can't guarantee that their children will grow up to be mentally healthy. This is difficult to believe, because parenting book authors, school counselors, and a host of other authorities have many parents convinced that the slightest mistake will cause permanent damage to their children. "Parents are nervous about doing the wrong thing, fearful that a stray word or glance might ruin their child's chances forever," says Judith Rich Harris, whose book *The Nurture Assumption* reviews a huge body of evidence showing that genetic factors and peer influence play a major role in children's behavior, while parenting styles have little or no effect (see Chapter 8). "Not only have they become servants to their children; they have been declared unsatisfactory servants, because the standards set by the promulgators of the nurture assumption are so high that no one can meet them."[12] If all of this angst resulted in happier, more successful children, then the professionals who promote the image of modern children as delicate beings capable of being irreparably damaged by a parental misstep would be doing society a favor. But it doesn't, because children aren't as emotionally delicate as the "experts" want us to believe.

> *Do you fret that a cross word, a minor disciplinary mistake, or a failure to provide adequate mental stimulation could ruin your child's future? If so, stop worrying, because there's evidence that even extreme child-rearing practices have remarkably little effect on later life.*
>
> *One example: When anthropologist Harold Orlansky studied Albanian children several decades ago, it was the custom in Albania to tie infants to a wooden cradle placed in the darkest corner of the room. Often parents threw a cloth over their babies' heads, preventing the infants from seeing their parents or the world around them. While such an approach seems barbaric to most of us, accustomed as we are to admonitions about nurturing and stimulating our infants, Orlansky found that the Albanian children's social behavior in later years equaled or surpassed that of Viennese children raised by more standard Western methods.[13]*
>
> *In related research in Guatemala, researcher Jerome Kagan studied children kept in dark huts during their early years, isolated and frequently ill or neglected. Expecting these children to be emotionally damaged, he was surprised to find that they grew up to be normal ten-year-olds with no emotional or mental scars.[14]*

Obviously, the lesson to be learned from research showing the limits of parental influence is not that we should stick our children in dark corners, neglect them, or abuse them—because even if our behavior has little effect on our children's futures, it most certainly affects the happiness of their lives today. Rather, the lesson is that, if even serious family dysfunction or extreme neglect has surprisingly little effect on how children function as adults, then blaming aberrant behavior on unhappy events occurring in childhood is simply nonsensical.

By the way, people skeptical about my conclusions will point to many studies showing that parents greatly influence their children's behavior. Those skeptics, however, should read a recent review article by John Paul Wright and Kevin Beaver. Studying the sociological literature, these two researchers noticed that many influential studies linking parental failings to low self-control in children (a risk factor for life problems and criminality) had serious design flaws. To test the effects of these flaws, Wright and Beaver first analyzed data on 1000 children using standard sociological methods, and found a strong link between parenting style and children's self-control. Next, using better data analysis methods and factoring in the role of genes (something sociological papers rarely do), they re-analyzed the same data. The result: parents had only a weak effect on their children's self-control—and close to no effect, when the researchers used data from teacher evaluations.[15] Their findings are consistent with Judith Rich Harris's conclusion, after reviewing massive numbers of sociologically oriented studies, that "the evidence developmental psychologists use to support the nurture assumption is not what it appears to be: it does not prove what it appears to prove."[16]

But if parents aren't responsible for our dyslogic epidemic, can we blame other sociological factors—poverty, for instance, and poor schools? Here, too, the evidence is less than convincing. While being poor clearly isn't good for children, programs to combat poverty have made little dent in dysfunctional behavior. In the four decades since Lyndon Johnson's War on Poverty, a wide range of highly touted liberal and conservative sociological interventions have been unveiled with great hope, tested for some years, and then found to cause small improvement in our rates of criminality and delinquency, drug and alcohol abuse, illiteracy, or school failure.

Efforts to improve school performance by increasing funding have had similarly little effect, as have efforts to change school curricula. Hundreds of different school reforms have been tried in past decades. Yet test scores only inch up (at best) and the numbers of learning disabled, hyperactive, and conduct disordered children continue to increase—more proof that there is more to the dyslogic epidemic than "nurture" alone can explain.

MYTH #2: NURTURE IS STRONGER THAN NATURE

This myth, a corollary of Myth #1, says that genes have almost nothing to do with who we are and what we accomplish. According to this myth, it doesn't matter if your dad is Albert Schweitzer or an axe murderer. You start with a clean slate the day you're born, and you have unlimited potential to succeed or fail.

It's a nice theory, and I wish it were true. Unfortunately, it's not even *close* to being true.

Moreover, we already know this instinctively. Dog owners know that most pit bulls are far more aggressive than cocker spaniels. Farmers know that pigs bred to be very lean often are so nervous that they are prone to have heart attacks and die during transport. Cattle ranchers use selective breeding to produce animals with mild temperaments. In each case, environment may play a role in how animals behave—for instance, a pit bull can be trained to be a vicious killer, or to be relatively peaceful—but environment won't change an animal's basic nature.

What's true of animals is also true of humans: studies show that your DNA plays more of a role in your personality and behavior than anything your mother and father do for (or to) you. You've probably read stories of identical twins, reunited after being separated at birth and raised under dramatically different circumstances, who share the same religious beliefs, hobbies, and even taste in clothes. Scientists once dismissed such tales as merely interesting coincidences, but studies of twins and of adoptive children have revealed the powerful role that genes play in molding everything from our IQs to our political views—and, of relevance to dyslogic, in influencing how well we think, how well we behave, how prone we are to developing depression or substance abuse disorders, and even whether or not we become criminals.

Powerful evidence of this comes from studies of people who are adopted at birth—thus getting their genes from one set of parents, and their nurturing (or lack of it) from an entirely different set of parents.

One of the most surprising of these studies showed that adopted men whose biological parents are criminals are *four times* more likely to become criminals than those whose biological parents aren't law-breakers.[17] Another study reported that biological parents have far more impact on whether adoptees commit property crimes than do adoptive parents.[18] Similarly, research shows that, when biological children of alcoholics are raised by non-alcoholic adoptive parents, their rate of alcoholism is roughly equal to that found in children of alcoholics raised by alcoholic parents.[19] Conversely, environmental factors such as psychiatric or alcohol problems in the adoptive family do *not* influence adoptee alcoholism.[20]

And remember I said that even extreme mistreatment has surprisingly little effect on how children do later in life? A few years ago, Avshalom Caspi and his coworkers made this point dramatically. Caspi and his team investigated the backgrounds of men participating in a long-term study, and identified 154 who'd been maltreated, some of them severely, as children. The researchers screened the formerly abused men to see which ones carried a high-activity variant of a particular gene, and which carried the low-activity variant. (The gene affects the function of MAOA, an enzyme that metabolizes several neurotransmitters.) They picked this gene because the low-activity variant is implicated as a culprit in abnormal aggression.

Comparing the high- and low-activity gene groups, Caspi and his team found that 85 percent of severely abused men with the low-activity gene variant developed some form of antisocial behavior. In contrast, study participants with the high-activity variant only rarely exhibited aggressive or criminal behavior as adults, even if they'd been severely abused as children.[21]

The researchers followed up this study with another, comparing identical twins (who share all of their genes) to fraternal twins (who share only half), a design that allowed Caspi and his team to determine what part genes played in determining which children developed conduct disorder. They reported, "The experience of maltreatment was associated with an increase of 2 percent in the probability of a conduct disorder diagnosis among children at low genetic risk for conduct disorder but an increase of 24 percent among children at high genetic risk." In other words, for almost all of the children in a bad environment, genes played the decisive role in determining whether or not the youngsters showed early signs of delinquent behavior.[22]

Again, this is *good* news, not bad news. Genes can predict vulnerability to dyslogical behavior, but they don't (except in rare cases) condemn an individual to a dismal fate. Does a child's genetic makeup affect his levels of neurotransmitters or hormones? Good. Then we can alter these levels. Do his genes make him susceptible to toxins or a bad diet? Then we can intervene, by removing the toxins or changing the diet. As I will discuss in greater length in Chapter 8, identifying genetic anomalies can point us in the direction of real, effective treatments for many cases of dyslogic.

My friend and fellow researcher William Walsh, who's had stunning success in treating antisocial children (more on his work in Chapter 8), says that identifying a genetic vulnerability in a child makes him happy—"because genes mean chemistry, and we can fix chemistry."[23] To fix that chemistry, however, we need to address it with biological treatments—not with psychological and sociological ones. Which brings us to...

MYTH #3: SOCIOLOGICAL AND PSYCHOLOGICAL INTERVENTIONS ARE EFFECTIVE IN TREATING DEVIANCY AND DYSLOGIC

Because we naively assume that dyslogical behavior stems solely from psychosocial causes, we address these behaviors almost exclusively with psycho-sociological interventions. Our efforts at prevention or rehabilitation of society's troubled souls generally focus on a) counseling and psychotherapy for troubled youths, b) education and counseling programs to deter "at risk" children from a life of crime or failure, and c) programs to combat poverty and other sociological risk factors for psychopathology.

Of all of these tools, the one we put most stock in is psychological therapy, including counseling and psychotherapy. We spend millions of dollars each year to counsel murderers, rapists, and robbers. We spend millions more to provide therapy for at-risk children and teens, and even more for counseling sessions for entire student bodies. We pull school children out of classes, sometimes on a weekly basis, to discuss their worries, take tests measuring their self-esteem, and air their real or perceived family problems.

The major problem with these approaches is simply this: they don't work.

I know that this statement will astonish many readers. Given the pervasive influence of counselors, psychologists, and psychiatrists in our society, most of us assume that psychological interventions are highly effective. The truth, however, is that decades of long-term and extensive research studies show that few of these programs have demonstrable positive effects, and some even have *negative* effects.

One of the best illustrations of this failure is in the area of prisoner rehabilitation. Many prison wardens, parole officers, judges, and even prison therapists privately admit that counseling and psychotherapy are generally ineffective in reducing rates of re-offending, and scientific research clearly supports this pessimistic view.

Take the case of Patuxent Institution, in Maryland. For decades, the facility focused its efforts on rehabilitation rather than punishment. Inmates received both individual and group psychotherapy to help them "understand the roots of their criminal behavior," and furloughs and paroles were based not on how much time prisoners served, but rather on how much supposed insight into their problems they gained. While Patuxent claimed its program was effective, a 1991 study showed that "former Patuxent inmates are just as likely to be rearrested as are people released from other state prisons included in the study," and that the intensive therapy had "no discernible effect" on future criminal behavior.[24]

Psychiatrist E. Fuller Torrey notes that Patuxent's experience isn't unusual. One review of 13 different studies, he says, concluded that therapy for prisoners yielded no clear-cut benefits—and that when behavioral therapies (which are somewhat successful) were excluded, and only psychoanalytic therapies were examined, treatment "is perhaps even harmful." Such findings bring to mind the comment by disillusioned psychotherapist Samuel Yocelson: "After psychotherapy, we have produced criminals with insight, but criminals nonetheless."[25]

But what if we catch at-risk children or young adults *before* they get into trouble? Can counseling and guidance set these at-risk individuals on a different path, steering them away from delinquency, substance abuse, and other dangerous behavior? Sadly, the answer appears to be no.

In one classic study, researchers divided nearly 400 "at-risk" girls into two groups on a random basis. Half the girls were counseled by social workers, while the other half received no intervention. The result: psychological intervention failed to produce any positive effects.[26]

Another highly publicized study, the Cambridge-Somerville Youth Study,[27] was by far the most extensive study of its kind, involving more than 500 delinquent and pre-delinquent youngsters from the Boston area and investigating both short-term and long-term effects of psychotherapy on troubled youths. The researchers conducting the study divided their subjects into an experimental group that received intensive and extensive counseling and psychotherapy, and a randomly matched control group that experienced no intervention. At the end of the original program, investigators were astonished to find that the psychotherapy-treated group had been involved in 264 offenses, while the untreated group committed only 218.

A long-term follow-up of the Cambridge-Somerville participants was even more startling. After 30 years, researchers located nearly 80 percent of the original participants in the study and evaluated their outcomes. Their findings were striking: on almost every measure, the follow-up found that the young men who'd been treated were significantly *worse off* than the controls! Further, the more intensive the treatment provided to members of the experimental groups, the worse they fared in comparison to the controls. Similar negative effects were reported in an Army study in which it was found that offenders provided with a supposedly "preventive" counseling program actually committed more offenses than those randomly assigned to an uncounseled control group.[28]

The same is often true of newer interventions, which typically don't fare any better than traditional psychotherapy. The much-touted "self-esteem" programs that hundreds of schools adopted in the early 1990s, for instance, proved to be an embarrassing failure—not a real surprise, when studies revealed that high-achieving students tend to have the lowest levels of self-esteem, and low-performing students the highest. Even well-constructed educational programs, such as the DARE anti-drug program, appear to have little or no effect in reducing levels of deviant behavior, despite the vast sums of money poured into these projects. And "Scared Straight," an ambitious program designed to expose at-risk children to the horrors of prison life and thereby turn them from a life of crime, also is a flop: in 1999, the National Youth Development Information Center reported that "'Scared Straight' programs which bring minor juvenile offenders to visit maximum security prisons do not reduce re-offending rates, and may actually increase crime."[29]*

Learning from our failures

What is the lesson here? While extremely bad environments may increase the odds that a child experiences problems in school or in life, crime and failure can't simply be blamed on bad parents, bad schools, or bad circumstances. Frequently, children overcome bad environments to become remarkable successes—and just as frequently, good parents and good circumstances fail to protect an individual from ruin. And all of our efforts at counseling, education, and therapy seem to have little or no effect on these disparate outcomes.

Why? Because solutions that focus only on "nurture" neglect "nature," and, more specifically, the brain itself. Yet the integrity of the brain ultimately determines our behavior, our thinking, and our ability to be moral, responsible, intelligent people. A child with a healthy

---

*   Of related interest: Counselors are typically rushed immediately to the scenes of disasters, such as terrorist attacks, earthquakes, or school shootings, to mitigate the post-traumatic psychological effects on the survivors. Nine thousand counselors were dispatched to New York, for instance, in the aftermath of the 9/11 attack. Such intervention, however, may actually do more harm than good. To quote a recent comprehensive review of studies on the efficacy of "psychological debriefing" (McNally et al., *Psychological Science in the Public Interest*, 2003): "[T]here is no convincing evidence that debriefing reduces the incidence of post traumatic stress disorder, and some controlled studies suggest that it may impede natural recovery from trauma. Most studies show that individuals who receive debriefing fare no better than those who do not receive debriefing."

brain is equipped to enjoy the pleasures of the world, confront its challenges, and cope with its tragedies. But a child with a damaged or dysfunctional brain is programmed for failure—no matter how many loving and well-meaning parents, teachers, and counselors attempt to change his fate—unless biological interventions can alter that course.

Notes

1 Cited by Torrey, E.F. in "Oedipal wrecks," *Washington Monthly 24*, Jan–Feb 1992, 1–2, 32–40.

2 Fact sheet, Voices for Children.

3 Hare, R. (1999) *Without Conscience: The Disturbing World of the Psychopaths Among Us*. New York: Guilford Press, p.171.

4 Rowe, D.C. (1994) *The Limits of Family Influence*. New York: Guilford Press, p.168.

5 Stevenson, I. (1957) "Is the human personality more plastic in infancy and childhood?" *American Journal of Psychiatry 114*, 152–61.

6 Gross, M. (1978) *The Psychological Society*. New York: Random House.

7 Macfarlane, J. (1964) "Perspectives on personality consistency and change from the guidance study." *Vita Humana 7*, 2, 115–26.

8 Renaud, H. and Estess, F. (1961) "Life history interviews with one hundred normal American males." *American Journal of Orthopsychiatry 31*, 786–802.

9 Study cited by Carter, R. in "Mapping the mind," *London Independent*, October 30, 1998.

10 Hare, R.D. (1999) *Without Conscience: The Disturbing World of the Psychopaths Among Us*. New York: Guilford Press, p.171.

11 Huh, D., Tristan, J., Wade, E. and Stice, E. (2006) "Does problem behavior elicit poor parenting? A prospective study of adolescent girls." *Journal of Adolescent Research 21*, 2, 185–204.

12 Harris, J.R. (1998) *The Nurture Assumption*. New York: Free Press, p.352.

13 Orlansky, H. (1949) "Infant care and personality." *Psychological Bulletin 46*, 1–48.

14 Cited by Leo, J. in "Lessons in Bringing Up Baby," *Time*, October 22, 1984.

15 Wright, J.P. and Beaver, K.M. (2005) "Do parents matter in creating self-control in their children? A genetically informed test of Gottfredson and Hirschi's theory of low self-control." *Criminology 43*, 4, 1169–202.

16 Harris, J.R. (1998) *The Nurture Assumption*. New York: Free Press, p.4.

17 Cloninger, C.R., Sigvardsson, S., Bohman, M. and von Knorring, A.-L. (1982) "Predisposition to petty criminality in Swedish adoptees." *Archives of General Psychiatry 39*, 1242–7, cited by William Walsh in "Chemical imbalances and criminal violence." Available at NOHA News, www.nutrition4health.org (accessed 10 October 2007)..

18   Mednick, S.A., Gabrielli, W.F. Jr. and Hutchings, B. (1994) "Genetic influences in criminal convictions: Evidence from an adoption cohort." *Science 224*, 4651, 891–4.

19   Goodwin, D.W. (1990) "Evidence for a genetic factor in alcoholism." In R. Engs (ed.) *Controversies in the Addictions Field*. Dubuque: Kendal-Hunt.

20   Cadoret, R.J., Cain, C.A. and Grove, W.M. (1980) "Development of alcoholism in adoptees raised apart from alcoholic biologic relatives." *Archives of General Psychiatry 37*, 5, 561–3.

21   Caspi, A., McClay, J., Moffitt, T., Mill, J., Martin, J., Craig, I.W., Taylor, A. and Poulton, R. (2002) "Role of genotype in the cycle of violence in maltreated children." *Science 297*, 851–4.

22   Jaffee, S.R., Caspi, A., Moffitt, T., Dodge, K.A., Rutter, M., Taylor, A. and Tully, L. (2005) "Nature x nurture: Genetic vulnerabilities interact with physical maltreatment to promote conduct problems." *Development and Psychopathology 17*, 67–84.

23   Personal communication.

24   Torrey, E.F. (1992) "Oedipal wrecks." *Washington Monthly 24*, Jan–Feb, 1–2, 32–40.

25   Yocelson, S. and Samenow, S. (1973) *The Criminal Personality*. New York: Jason Aronson.

26   Meyer, H.J., Borgatta, E.F. and Jones, K.L. (1965) *Girls at Vocational High: An Experiment in Social Work Intervention*. New York: Russell Sage.

27   McCord, J. (1978) "A thirty-year follow-up of treatment effects." *American Psychologist 33*, 284–9.

28   Bell, D.B. and Holz, R.F. (1975) "Summary of ARI research on military delinquency." RR1185, Alexandria, VA, Army Research Institute, June.

29   "Preventing crime: What's promising and what isn't," National Youth Development Information Center, 1999.

CHAPTER 4

Why Drugs Don't Cure Dyslogic

"The sole purpose of psychotropic drugs is to suppress symptoms. But a symptom is a signal that something is wrong, and ignoring or suppressing it won't make the problem go away."

—Sydney Walker III, M.D.[1]

In the last chapter, I explained why sociological cures for dyslogic typically don't work. Luckily, society is gradually beginning to realize that blaming parents won't solve the problems of America's troubled children. Just as doctors finally stopped blaming autism and schizophrenia on bad mothers, they are gradually beginning to recognize that psychosocial factors don't sufficiently explain dyslogic, and that psychosocial fixes won't effectively prevent or treat it.

One reason for this new awareness is that, at the dawn of the twenty-first century, medicine is in the first stages of a "brain revolution." This revolution began a few decades ago, when doctors were forced to stop blaming severe mental illnesses on bad parenting, and instead started blaming these disorders correctly on malfunctioning brains. It progressed as science revealed the biological underpinnings of depression and anxiety. And it will continue as physicians grow to realize that crime, delinquency, violence, oppositional behavior, and school failure also are largely *biomedical* problems that need to be addressed with biomedical treatments—not psycho-sociological problems that can be addressed by counseling and psychotherapy.

Indeed, this change in doctors' attitudes about dyslogic is already underway. Most doctors now recognize that hyperactivity, depression, and attention deficit disorder, once blamed on poor parenting, are disorders caused by brain dysfunction. The medical community is coming to grips with evidence showing that biology plays a huge role in behavior and personality and, by extension, in behavioral aberrations. Simultaneously, brain scans, biochemical studies, and other technologies are providing clear evidence that the brains of troubled, learning disabled, and criminal children are indeed different from healthy brains.

As a result, growing numbers of doctors who treat "difficult" children and young adults no longer automatically think, "What's wrong with this kid's parents?" Instead, many are now beginning to ask, "What's wrong with this kid's brain?" While educators, the criminal justice system, and the public still tend to believe almost universally that behavior problems stem from bad schools or bad parents, medical practitioners are gradually becoming aware that problems in the brain lead to problems in behavior, and that treatments for these problems must address the brain itself.

There's only one drawback to this change in attitude: most medical doctors, trained to fix every ill with a pill, tend to equate biomedical treatments with drugs. Thus, when they stop sending troubled children to psychiatrists and psychologists for talk therapy, they simply start writing them prescriptions instead. As a consequence, millions of young Americans, ranging from fidgety school children to hard-core delinquents, are now taking powerful mind-altering drugs.

In some cases, there's no viable alternative to these drugs. There are children who can't be helped with any treatments that we currently have, and drugs have a place in treating these children. But what parents aren't being told is that drug treatments need to be a last resort, not a first choice. As I explain in later chapters, doctors are failing to inform parents that, for many if not most dyslogical children, we have safe and effective alternatives.

But why *not* reach for a pill as a first option, if drugs can reduce a dyslogical child's symptoms quickly? Because psychiatric drugs often come with a high price tag: they make many children sick, and kill some of them. In fact, these drugs can be much more dangerous than the failed psychological treatments they're replacing.

> *When Mark Miller's 13-year-old son Matt had trouble adjusting to a new school after his family moved, and his grades started slipping, his school counselors recommended professional help. Matt's physician, in turn, recommended Zoloft. "Our doctor simply said try these pills for a week," Miller says. But he adds, "We didn't have a week."*
>
> *A few days after starting on Zoloft, Matt became extremely restless, "hyper," and agitated—a dangerous drug side effect called akathisia, sometimes associated with violent acts. That night, he hanged himself in his closet. "He did not leave a note," his father says. "He had never threatened suicide. He never talked about it. He indicated in his doctor's office just a week before, he would never consider suicide an option. He never gave us any indication that he had been thinking about it. I honestly don't believe he had thought about it, until something happened inside his tortured mind that night."*
>
> *Miller's father later discovered that emotional swings, mania, agitation, anxiety, and hyperactive behavior were among the adverse effects seen in clinical trials of Zoloft. Unfortunately, he says, he wasn't warned about these potential dangers when Matt got his prescription. "Our veterinarian gave us five pages of information on medication prescribed for our dog's stomach problems," he says. "We received nothing that would help us understand Zoloft."[2]*

Cases like Matt's led the Food and Drug Administration to add a "black box" warning to the packaging of Zoloft and other antidepressants, cautioning doctors that these drugs can cause suicidal thoughts or actions in children. Nonetheless, doctors in the U.S. continue to prescribe Zoloft to pediatric patients.

Why are drugs the only biological treatment that most doctors offer? Because, while doctors are increasingly willing to believe that dyslogic stems from brain dysfunction, far too few doctors are well informed as to *why* children's brains become dyslogical. Adding to the problem, cost-cutting HMOs and other managed care programs encourage quick fixes, rather than appropriate treatments for behavioral problems.

It's true, too, that drugs often are effective, *in the short term*, in quelling aggressive, oppositional, or hyperactive behavior. Psychiatric drugs can make the learning disabled or hyperactive child calmer—at least temporarily. They can sedate the out-of-control delinquent—at least temporarily. And they can make the troublesome child less difficult—at least temporarily. But drugs are a temporary fix: they mask symptoms, for a while, but fail to correct their causes. Giving a troubled child Prozac or Ritalin is much like giving a child with a brain tumor a pain pill: you may make the child seem better, and reduce the stress on his family and teachers, for a little while, but the destructive processes wreaking havoc on his brain won't magically go away.

Drugs may be necessary in cases where no other approaches work, and I certainly don't fault parents for using medications in these circumstances. The people I do fault are the doctors who tout these medications as wonder drugs, and prescribe them as the front-line treatment for dyslogical children, without discussing their drawbacks or offering safe alternatives. Here's a look at the damage this approach is doing to an entire generation.

Stimulants: an epidemic of over-drugging

Visit a doctor with your hyperactive, attention-disordered or learning disabled child, and it's a good bet that you'll be handed a prescription for stimulant drugs. These drugs typically fall into two categories: the methylphenidate drugs such as Ritalin, Concerta, Methylin, and Metadate, and amphetamine drugs such as Adderall, Dextrostat, Dexedrine, and Desoxyn.

Doctors write more than 30 million prescriptions for stimulant drugs each year, and consider them the front-line treatment for attention deficit hyperactivity disorder (ADHD) and similar problems. And it's true that stimulants can be a "quick fix." The drugs do slow down many hyperactive children. At least initially, they may allow kids to pay attention in class, make them easier to manage at home, and give their parents and teachers relief from their exhausting behavior. So what's the problem?

First of all, stimulants can be dangerous. Their dangers came to light recently when a panel convened by the Food and Drug Administration recommended that Ritalin and other drugs for ADHD carry a black box warning—the strongest warning possible for pharmaceuticals.[3]

The panel based its recommendation on an FDA review which uncovered 25 sudden deaths due to cardiac arrest involving children and adults taking stimulant drugs between 1999 and 2003. The same review identified 54 non-fatal cases of heart attack, stroke, hypertension, arrhythmia, or heart palpitations in patients taking these drugs. Doctors who spoke to the panel noted that stimulant drugs increase blood pressure and heart rate, and that preliminary data suggest that the drugs increase the risk of strokes and arrhythmias. Dr. David Graham commented, "The number of arrhythmia hospitalizations really struck us as surprising. Arrhythmia is believed to be the pathway for sudden unexplained death."[4]

Current data, panel members noted, suggest that stimulant drugs more than double the risk of heart problems. In fact, statistician Thomas Fleming told the *New York Times*, the drugs may prove to be more dangerous than Vioxx, the arthritis drug removed from the market in 2004 due to its link to strokes and heart attacks. Drug safety expert Andrew Mosholder noted that the chemical structures of stimulants resemble those of ephedrine, the diet drug banned after it caused several fatalities.

This information, and the "black box" recommendation that followed, shocked many people. However, while some of the findings are new, the dangers of stimulant drugs are well known. The *Physicians' Desk Reference* (which, it should be noted, is produced by the drug industry itself) notes that the drug can lower seizure thresholds, sometimes provoking seizures in individuals with no prior electroencephalogram (EEG) abnormalities or histories of seizures, and can cause cardiac arrhythmia, tic disorders, loss of appetite, abdominal pain, temporary weight loss and stunted growth, insomnia, and a long list of other unpleasant or dangerous reactions. In addition, it can cause toxic psychosis, in which children experience hallucinations and delirium.

As for Adderall, its side effects include paranoia, elevated suspiciousness and nervousness, high blood pressure, rapid pulse, loss of appetite, tremor, depression, and addiction—to list just a sampling. The *Physicians' Desk Reference* also notes that "tolerance, extreme psychological dependence, and severe social disability" have been reported in patients taking the drug. Its cardiac effects are more dangerous than those of Ritalin, and the Canadian government, reviewing the evidence against Adderall, banned the drug in 2005.

And what about Strattera, a newer non-stimulant drug for ADHD? In 2005, the FDA directed Strattera's manufacturer to add a warning that the drug can increase the risk of suicidal thinking in children.[5] It also causes a host of other side effects, including nausea, vomiting, liver damage, weakness, and fatigue.

If your doctor tries to write a prescription for any of these drugs, consider their potential risks, and to try other solutions—like the much more effective ones I'll outline later—before you think about saying "yes."

Antidepressants: the real risk/benefit profile

Ritalin, once the drug of choice for problem children, is now just one item in a pharmaceutical grab-bag that also includes a growing number of antidepressants—chief among them the selective serotonin reuptake inhibitors, or SSRIs, such as Paxil, Zoloft, Celexa, and Luvox. Doctors prescribe these drugs for millions of children but they can be very dangerous, and there is little evidence for their long-term effectiveness—particularly in pediatric patients. Says Jane Garland, head of the Mood and Anxiety Disorders Clinic at Children's Hospital in Vancouver, "The disappointing reality is that antidepressant medications have minimal to no effectiveness in childhood depression beyond a placebo effect."[6]

The failure of antidepressants to help troubled children would be less damning if it weren't for these drugs' harmful or even potentially lethal side effects. But many parents find that within weeks (or sometimes even hours) of starting on the drugs, their children become depressed, agitated, violent, or even suicidal. Among the cases making the news:

- A bright, artistic graduate of Stanford University, Cecily Bostock started taking Paxil for anxiety and sleep problems. She immediately grew agitated and began exhibiting bizarre behavior. Less than three weeks later, she stabbed herself to death in her parents' kitchen.[7]

- Seventeen-year-old Julie Woodward had a little trouble fitting in when she moved from a small girl's school to a large high school. A doctor recommended Zoloft to reduce her stress, saying it was mild and very safe. Seven days after starting the drug, Julie—who'd never been depressed or exhibited any suicidal tendencies—hanged herself in the family's garage."[8]

- When Caitlin McIntosh started sixth grade and reached puberty, she had trouble coping and developed sleep problems. A doctor put her on Paxil, then switched her to Zoloft. She began hallucinating, developed severe agitation, and was placed in a mental hospital to "balance her meds" (with yet more drugs). Shortly after she came home, she hanged herself in the girl's bathroom at her school.[9]

By 2003, the evidence linking antidepressants to suicidal or other aberrant behavior in children was so alarming that the British government banned the use of six of these drugs for pediatric patients. In 2004, the U.S. Food and Drug Administration's *own experts* testified at a public hearing that the drugs are largely ineffective, and can increase the risk of suicidal behavior. In response, the FDA, after a month's delay, issued a warning to doctors, and asked antidepressant manufacturers to put similar warnings on their labels. However, the drugs are still widely prescribed for children and teens.

The suicidal or violent behavior seen in some children taking antidepressants is terrifying, but it's not the only side effect of these drugs. Another is that antidepressants, while considered non-addictive, can cause serious withdrawal symptoms. SSRIs can also cause "serotonin syndrome," a potentially dangerous condition with symptoms that

How good a track record do antidepressants and Ritalin have, when it comes to treating dyslogical or "crazy" behavior? Consider this list of children who made headlines for committing violent crimes:

- T. J. Solomon, 15 years old, wounded six children at Heritage High School in Conyers, Georgia. He was taking Ritalin at the time.

- Sixteen-year-old Jeff Weisse, who shot ten people dead in Red Lake, Minnesota, before killing himself, was on Prozac at the time of his rampage.

- Eric Harris, one of the teens who killed 13 people at Columbine High, had been taking the antidepressant Luvox and had a "therapeutic level" of the drug in his body at the time of the massacre.

- Kip Kinkel, who shot four children and wounded 23 in Springfield, Oregon, had been taking Prozac and Ritalin.

- Jeremy Strohmeyer, who raped and murdered a seven-year-old girl, was on Dexedrine, a drug similar to Ritalin.

- Michael Carneal, a 14-year-old who shot eight teens at a school prayer meeting, was reportedly taking Ritalin.

- Fifteen-year-old Shawn Cooper, who opened fire with a shotgun at his Idaho school, was on Ritalin.

- Fourteen-year-old Rod Mathews, who beat a classmate to death with a baseball bat, had taken Ritalin since third grade.

- James Wilson, 19, who killed two girls and wounded seven other children and two teachers at a South Carolina school, had taken psychotropic drugs for five years.

- Ben Garris, a 16-year-old who stabbed his counselor to death, was on antidepressants.
- 16-year-old Jarred Viktor stabbed his grandmother 61 times. Ten days earlier, Jarred had started taking the antidepressant Paxil.
- Kristine Fetters, a 14-year-old who stabbed her beloved great-aunt, was being treated with antidepressants.

Clearly, these drugs aren't a panacea when it comes to stopping troubled children and teens from committing violent acts—and given the large numbers of such acts we're now seeing, compared to the minuscule number in the decades before psychiatric drug use became rampant, we must consider the possibility that a significant number of violent acts occur as a result of—not in spite of—the drugs our children are taking.

include confusion, agitation, abnormal heartbeat, seizures, fever, pain, and, in some cases, coma and death. And traditional tricyclics, a different type of antidepressants, have plenty of side effects as well. One is sudden death due to cardiac arrest, a phenomenon that can occur in children as well as adults.

Antipsychotics: diabetes and other risks

One recent addition to the doctors' arsenal is a category of drugs called "atypical antipsychotics." These drugs are called "atypical" because they're different from older psychiatric drugs such as Thorazine and Mellaril, and they're called "antipsychotics" because they're supposedly intended for people with severe psychoses, such as schizophrenia. The truth, however, is that the drugs are also being given to thousands of children with conduct disorder, ADHD, and other behavior and learning problems.

THE LITHIUM EXCEPTION

It's interesting that lithium, used successfully to treat bipolar disorder (manic depression), is the one antidepressant that's proven to be effective both in reducing symptoms and in lowering suicide risk. Lithium is actually not a drug, but rather a naturally occurring mineral found in trace amounts in the human body. In fact, some experts regard lithium as a nutrient—that is, a substance essential for the body. While lithium has side effects, its risk/benefit ratio is vastly superior to many other psychiatric medications.

In addition to its usefulness in treating bipolar disorder, lithium is one of the few substances that also can be effective in lowering the aggression of violent criminals. In fact, it may help to prevent criminal behavior in the first place: lithium occurs naturally in the water supply in many areas, and research indicates that rates of homicide, suicide, rape, robbery, burglary, theft, and arrests for possession of opium and cocaine are higher in areas where the drinking water contains little or no lithium than in counties with naturally high water lithium levels.[10]

Thus, lithium must be considered not as a success story for pharmaceuticals, but rather as an example of how we can restore healthy brain functioning by providing the brain with naturally occurring nutrients rather than artificial chemicals.

Although these drugs—Risperdal, Clozaril, Seroquel, Zyprexa, and others—are relatively new and little-tested on children, doctors began prescribing them immediately and indiscriminately when they first came on the market. And equally quickly, their patients, including children, began falling ill. That's because atypical antipsychotics can cause dangerous fluctuations in blood sugar, with results that are catastrophic or potentially even fatal. The drugs also can cause diabetes, even in children. (One recent case involved a seven-year-old boy.) They often cause massive weight gain, too, putting children at risk for both health problems and social stigmatization. In addition, patients taking antipsychotics may develop pancreatitis or pituitary tumors, or experience a condition called "long QT syndrome," a cardiac abnormality that can lead to sudden death.

Asked to list the most dangerous current drugs, David Graham —the FDA whistleblower who "outed" the FDA for covering up the dangers of Vioxx, later withdrawn from the market—cited Risperdal, a very popular atypical antipsychotic, as one of the worst. Yet doctors prescribe more than 6 billion dollars' worth of Risperdal and other antipsychotics each year, and the numbers are growing annually.

Why many doctors fail their patients

Why do doctors rarely warn patients adequately about the dangerous side effects of the drugs used to treat dyslogical children? Partly because they're often poorly informed themselves. Doctors have little training in pharmacology, and they obtain much of their information from pharmaceutical company representatives—or from the FDA, which is currently under fire for downplaying or even trying to conceal the risks of prescription drugs because of its strong ties to the drug industry.

Also, there's no good system for tracking and reporting drug side effects. Studies show that as many as a million Americans are injured each year by prescription drugs, and about 60,000 die as a result of drug side effects,[11] but only a fraction of cases are actually reported by doctors. Additionally, HMOs put time pressures on doctors, who are now expected to limit office visits to just a few minutes. This means that physicians barely have time to write a prescription for a drug, much less tell patients how dangerous that drug can be.

This lack of information is particularly tragic when children are involved, because children are at even greater risk of crippling or fatal drug side effects than adults. Most drugs given to children never undergo long-term testing for safety in pediatric patients, and doctors often calculate children's doses by sheer guesswork, extrapolating from adult doses and ignoring the fact that children aren't simply little adults.

Adding to the danger, doctors often try to treat drug side effects such as insomnia or anxiety by adding still more medications to create a "drug cocktail." Unfortunately, these drugs can combine in unexpected and often dangerous ways, especially in the vulnerable bodies and brains of children. "I can tell you anecdotally," the late Sydney Walker, M.D., wrote, "that patients on three, four, or even more psychiatric drugs are almost invariably a mess when they arrive at my office. At some point, their previous doctors' goal stopped being 'cure the patient' and simply became 'alleviate the effects of the last drug by adding more drugs'—a game that can't be won."[12]

Yet despite all of the dangers of drugging millions of children, physicians appear to consider drugs as the front-line treatment for any childhood behavior problem rather than as a last resort when other approaches fail. Lawrence Diller, M.D., commented in 2002, "Today these doctors appear to be pushing pills exclusive of anything else. In fact, a recent survey of child psychiatry practices by the Yale Child Study Center…revealed that only one in ten children who visit a child psychiatrist's office leaves without a psychiatric drug prescription."[13]

Orthomolecular vs. toximolecular treatment

In the chapters that follow, I will explain why the best and safest way to prevent mental and physical disorders, including "dyslogic," and to treat such disorders when they do occur, is through the use of natural substances that normally participate in the body's functioning. Such substances include, but are not limited to, vitamins, minerals, proteins, and essential fatty acids.

This concept, which makes obvious sense, was developed by my friend, the late Linus Pauling, the only person in history to win two unshared Nobel Prizes. Pauling, who is considered to be one of the greatest scientists of all time, referred to his idea as "orthomolecular medicine." The prefix "ortho" means correct or proper, and "molecular" refers to the chemistry of the body. By orthomolecular medicine, Pauling meant correcting the body's natural chemistry, primarily by using nutrients, all of which are inherently *helpful* to the body's metabolism.

Pauling's orthomolecular medicine presents a radical departure from the approach used in conventional medicine, which relies very heavily on drugs—chemicals foreign to the body which work by *blocking or interfering with* our metabolism. (That is why drugs are so often harmful.) Pauling's concept was rejected and ridiculed by mainstream medicine, because physicians are typically trained in the use of drugs ("medicines") and not nutrients. However, it has been taken to heart by a growing number of physicians who recognize the wisdom of working with, rather than against, the body's natural processes.

I have often discussed Pauling's concepts in my lectures to various groups, during which I contrast the two approaches toward attaining and maintaining health: Pauling's concept of orthomolecular medicine, which involves giving substances normally present in the body, versus the approach of drug-oriented conventional doctors. I characterize the latter approach as "toximolecular medicine."

"Toximolecular medicine," I say, "unlike orthomolecular medicine, is the attempt to attain health, or to maintain health, by giving sub-lethal doses of toxic substances." This characterization of conventional medicine initially shocks most audiences, but when they stop to consider my words, they realize that the description is accurate. Virtually 100 percent of drugs listed in the *Physicians' Desk Reference* (PDR) list death as a potential side effect, and death and illness from taking prescription drugs are commonplace. In contrast, significant adverse effects from overdosing on nutrients are virtually unheard of.

The drugs that doctors currently give to children suffering from dyslogic are toximolecular, because they fail to treat these children's true problems, while all too often causing crippling or even life-threatening side effects such as mania, suicidality, or homicidal rages. Brains aren't meant to be bathed in the artificial chemicals that drug companies manufacture, any more than they're meant to be bathed in the street drugs that prescription psychoactive drugs often resemble.

Of course, most doctors will tell you that suppressing symptoms with drugs is the best we can do when it comes to treating hyperactive, attention-disordered, learning disabled, conduct disordered, or otherwise dyslogical individuals, because "no one knows" what causes dyslogical behavior. In some cases, they're right—but in many cases, they're wrong. As I'll explain in the following chapters, we *do* know a great deal about the causes of dyslogic, and, what's more, we know of safe, effective orthomolecular treatments that address these root causes. Moreover, many doctors across America are already using these treatments to give troubled, learning disabled, or dangerous children a second chance at life.

Notes

1 Walker, S. (1996) *Dose of Sanity.* New York: John Wiley & Sons, p.55.

2 Miller's story is posted at the website of the International Coalition for Drug Awareness. Available at www.drugawareness.org (accessed 10 October 2007).

3 Harris, G. (2006) "Warning urged on stimulants like Ritalin." *New York Times,* February 10.

4 Ibid.

.5 "FDA issues public health advisory on Strattera (Atomoxetine) for Attention Deficit Disorder," September 29, 2005. Available at www.fda.gov/bbs/topics/NEWS/2005/NEW01237.html (accessed 26 September 2007).

6. Garland, J. (2004) "Facing the evidence: Antidepressant treatment in children and adolescents." *Canadian Medical Association Journal 170, 4*, February 17. Available at www.cmaj.cgi/content/full/170/4/489 (accessed 26 September 2007).

7 Details of Cecily Bostock's case are from an online interview at Carte Blanche Interactive, available at www.antidepressants.facts.com/2004-07-18-CB-antidep-your-problem.htm (accessed 4 October 2007), and S. Dentzer (2004) "Fighting Depression?", Public Broadcasting System, 28 May. Available at www.pbs.org/newshour/bb/health/jan-june04/depression_5-28.html)accessed 4 October 2007).

8 Details of Julie Woodward's case are taken from the *Philadelphia Inquirer Online.* Available at www.antidepres-sants.com/2003-07-22-Julie-Woodward-17-zoloft.htm (accessed 4 October 2007).

9 Details of Caitlin McIntosh's case are taken from the testimony of her father, Glenn McIntosh, before an FDA hearing on 2 February 2004. Available at www.fda.gov/OHRMS/DOCKETS/AC/04/transcripts/4006T1.htm (accessed 5 October 2007).

10 Schrauzer, G.N. and Shrestha, K.P. (1990) "Lithium in drinking water and the incidences of crimes, suicides and arrests related to drug addictions." *Biological Trace Element Research 25*, 2, 105–13.

11 Moore, T.J. (1998) *Prescription for Disaster.* New York: Dell.

12 Walker, S. *The Sad Neuron*, in press.

13 Diller, L. (2002) "A prescription for disaster." *Salon*, May 23.

PART II

The Dyslogic Culprits

The environmental, dietary, and medical causes of our
children's dysfunctional thinking and behavior

Dietary Dyslogic: Why What Your Kids Eat (or Don't Eat) Can Make Them Crazy, Sad, or Violent

"Garbage in, garbage out."

—Common saying of software programmers

Every thought, whether it's a logical thought ("I need to take out the trash") or a dyslogical thought ("I need to kill that man and steal his car"), begins in the brain. But how does your brain build a thought? Everything the brain does begins with the raw materials you put into it: the air you breathe, the water you drink, and, last but far from least, the food you eat.

It may seem odd that your actions and behavior stem, in part, from last night's pot roast or the salad you ate for lunch. But it's true, because food provides the nutrients that build everything from your brain cells to the chemicals they use to transmit messages. Your brain and your gut are exquisitely interconnected, and what you eat has a lot to do with how well you think.

Unfortunately, a lot can go wrong between your mouth and your brain. Sometimes problems start from within, with a malfunctioning digestive tract, a brain that requires an unusually large supply of some nutrients, or an immune system that can't deal with certain foods or food additives. More often, "dietary dyslogic" stems from a poor diet, usually combined with inborn vulnerabilities. As I'll explain later in this chapter, the typical American diet is custom-made to create dyslogic, because it's stripped of nutrients and pumped full of non-nutrients and even "anti-nutrients" such as sugar, additives, preservatives, and artificial colorings, which can impair brain function even in the healthiest of children.

The brain, it is often said, is a computer. Unlike your laptop or desktop computer, however, the brain is a *soggy* computer, consisting of about 85 percent water. The brain is really a soup, where messages are sent back and forth by means of substances dissolved in the soup. To work properly, the soup must consist of the right substances, in the correct amounts. These substances include vitamins, minerals, amino acids, and fatty acids. Even a slight shortage of any one will lead to trouble in a susceptible brain, and a significant shortage will lead to trouble in *any* brain. Conversely, as I'll explain in this chapter and the next, too much of the wrong stuff—additives, colorings, "junk foods," or toxins such as alcohol or heavy metals—will cause the brain to malfunction, and behavior will suffer as a result.

Any discussion of the brain/diet connection, however, begs an obvious question. We all know people who live on coffee, doughnuts, french fries, and takeout pizza, and, for the most part, these people don't drop out of school, develop psychiatric illnesses, or go berserk and kill their friends or spouses. Thus, there must be another piece to the nutrition/behavior puzzle. Why do some people react dyslogically—and often with violence—to a typical diet that doesn't cause markedly aberrant behavior in others?

The reason lies largely in our genetic makeup. Every human body is unique, making many of us far more vulnerable to nutritional stressors than others. Thus, one child, while never reaching his or her full potential, can remain at least marginally happy and healthy even while eating a diet that's low in nutrients and high in additives, while the same diet can leave another child sad, sick, or even homicidal. My own work has shown that high doses of vitamin B6 and magnesium frequently cause dramatic improvement in autistic children, who often need massive amounts of this vitamin. The work of respected physician Abram Hoffer, a friend of mine, demonstrated that many schizophrenics recover when given megadoses of vitamin B3 (see Chapter 8).

Does this mean that everyone requires megadoses of vitamin B6 or vitamin B3 to think and behave logically? No. It means that everyone's nutritional needs are unique, and that a diet that's adequate for one person can increase the risk of mental and behavioral problems—up to and including psychosis—in another. On paper, bureaucrats can create recommended daily values—the amounts of vitamins, minerals, and other nutrients that the government decrees are healthy and necessary for the "average" human being. But these simplistic guidelines overlook the obvious fact that the "average" person they're designed for doesn't exist. Instead, there are millions of us with very different nutritional needs, and vastly different vulnerabilities to deficiency.[1] For example:

- zinc levels can range from 1.2 to 11.4 micrograms per cubic centimeter of blood in healthy individuals

- vitamin A levels can vary ten-fold in normal people

- rates of vitamin C absorption in healthy athletes can vary up to ten times.[2]

As a result of such differences, even people eating healthful diets (and as I'll discuss shortly, such people are far rarer than you think) can be grossly deficient in nutrients crucial to the functioning of their brain. In many cases, these deficiencies lead to subclinical, easy-to-overlook brain dysfunction that translates into hyperactivity, poor attention, irritability, depression, mania, or learning or memory problems. In other cases, an undetected need for higher-than-typical levels of nutrients can lead to behavior that is markedly irrational or even life-threatening.

Dyslogic and "dysnutrition"

Individual differences, however, aren't the only (or even the primary) culprits in dietary dyslogic. While genetic diversity means that some of us require higher levels of certain nutrients, all of us need at least a minimal (for us) supply of every nutrient in order to think clearly and behave rationally.

Unfortunately, the raw materials most Americans provide for their brains are of poor grade, and consistently getting worse. Getting *enough* food isn't a problem for the overwhelming majority of Americans. It's *what* we eat that's the problem.

In the mid-1990s, Appleton Central Alternative High School in Wisconsin had a bad reputation—and with good reason. One administrator who turned down a job there, after a visit, stated that the students were "rude, obnoxious, very crude, and ill-mannered." The school had a full-time police officer who says, "I was brought over because the school was out of control. They were having a lot of problems with rebellious students, weapons violations—things of that nature."

Searching for new ways to help Central's students, Principal LuAnn Coenen turned to a company called National Ovens, which offered to replace the school's heavily junk-food-laden breakfast and lunch program with a menu of healthful whole grains, fruits, vegetables, and low-fat, low-sugar foods. Overnight, out went the soda machines and doughnuts; in went a salad bar, energy drinks, whole-grain bagels, and healthful hot lunches.

Since the program began, Coenen says, "I've seen a total change in the students and the environment within the school. It's amazing... Every year, we are required to file a state report. On that state report, we include information regarding the number of dropouts, expulsions, drugs, weapons, and suicides. Since we started the program, all three years, 'zero' is what I had to report. That's a pretty nice report to fill out."

Greg Bretthauer, the administrator who had initially turned down the job at Central, is now the dean of students, and he says, "I was hesitant to start but I found that the atmosphere is entirely different. The students are calm, they're well behaved, I don't have to deal with the daily discipline issues." Teacher Mary Bruyette agrees, saying, "Our biggest problems at this school right now are parking and school tardiness." She adds, "I think that I've been able to demand more academically from my students over the last few years than I could when we first opened the school… [Now] I use all of the minutes in the class period for instruction."

The program is such a success that Appleton is expanding it to other high schools, middle schools, and elementary schools. Says school district superintendent Dr. Thomas Scullen, "We believed that it would help settle the kids down, which it has done, but I think we were surprised at the impact that it's had on academic learning." Like the alternative school students, typical high school kids are responding to the change: says a science teacher at Madison Middle School, "I've been teaching here for almost 30 years…the kids this year seem calmer, they're easier to talk to, they just seem more rational. I'd thought about retiring this year, but I've decided to teach another year because I'm having too much fun." [3]

Appleton was one of the first school districts to implement a system-wide "healthy diet" program, but it wasn't the first to discover the differences between well-fed and ill-fed kids. Among other findings:

- Back in 1979, Stephen Schoenthaler analyzed the effects of a low-sugar diet introduced in 803 New York City schools, and introduced in stages over the next three years (the fourth year was unchanged from the previous year). Before the diet began, almost no change in achievement test scores occurred from one year to the next—and what little change occurred was usually negative. But over the next four years, as the diet was implemented, New York City public schools raised their mean national academic performance percentile ranking by 15.7 percent! Schoenthaler notes that these academic gains "propelled New York City schools from 11 percent below the national average to 5 percent above the mean."[4]

- In Wales, U.K., psychologist David Benton and educator Gwilyn Roberts, also interested in the relationship between

good food and children's "smarts," conducted a
placebo-controlled trial to determine if supplementing the
diets of students would improve their intelligence. It did:
after eight months, the IQ tests of the subjects taking the
supplements revealed an average gain of nine points in
non-verbal IQ.[5]

Other studies show that nutritional supplements can dramatically
improve the behavior of children, and hint that much of what we label
as attention deficit hyperactivity disorder (ADHD) is caused or exacer-
bated by nutritional deficiencies. Among the findings:

- Researchers comparing the effectiveness of Ritalin,
  megadoses of vitamin B6, and a placebo in treating
  hyperactive boys shown to be "responders" to Ritalin found
  that both the Ritalin and the B6 proved better than the
  placebo, but the B6 was better and longer lasting.[6] A more
  recent study, by a different research group, came to similar
  conclusions.[7] And French researcher Marianne
  Mousain-Bosc, who's treated nearly 140 ADHD children
  with a combination of B6 and magnesium, reports that the
  nutrients reduce the children's hyperactivity, agitation, and
  aggression, while improving their school performance.[8]

- Researchers in Britain gave supplements of essential fatty
  acids to 117 schoolchildren with developmental
  coordination disorder (a syndrome involving clumsiness
  and motor delays, often seen in children with other
  learning or behavioral problems). The researchers say
  children taking the supplements made more than nine
  months' worth of progress in reading during the first three
  months of treatment, compared to only three months of
  progress for a placebo group. At the beginning of the
  study, about one-third of the children had symptoms
  suggestive of ADHD, but half of the children taking the
  fatty acids improved so much that they no longer appeared
  to have ADHD.[9]

The dramatic change in students' performance and behavior when they take supplements or eat healthier food isn't surprising, when you consider the terrible diet consumed by today's children and teens. Not long ago, the National Cancer Institute investigated the diets of more than 3000 American children, and what the researchers found shocked them: of children between ages 2 and 19, *only 1 percent* met all of the Institute's standards for a decent diet. Worse yet, 16 percent of these children didn't meet *any* of the Institute's recommendations. Nearly half of the children's calories came from fats and added sugars, which are virtually barren of nutritional value.[10] The Department of Agriculture came to a similarly dismal conclusion when it analyzed children's diets: it found that "most children ages 2 to 9 have a diet that needs improvement or is poor," and that, as children age, their diets get increasingly more deficient.[11]

"Nutrition research surveys in the last two decades have shown that Americans are eating anything but balanced diets, and also uncovered three startling facts," physician Joseph Beasley writes in *The Betrayal of Health*. "One, there is clear-cut malnutrition in America among certain groups. Two, there are widespread deficiencies in several nutrients among the population at large. And three, these deficiencies are affecting our health, disease resistance, and performance—including school behavior and achievement."[12]

The explanation for this bizarre phenomenon—widespread poor nutrition, in a nation that produces a huge variety of foods—is actually fairly simple. Up until the middle 1800s, America's biggest nutritional problems were warding off actual starvation and keeping food from spoiling. With technological developments ranging from flour milling to the mass production and mass marketing of foods, we've nearly eliminated those problems. In the process, however, we've created a host of new and even more serious ones.

As a result of modern food manufacturing processes, we now eat a diet almost entirely divorced from nutritional reality. The bulk of our diet consists of highly refined white flour (a food unknown before the 1860s), sugar, and unhealthful forms of fats. Furthermore, we now process even good foods to the point that many are nutritionally almost worthless. As researcher Robert Harris of the Massachusetts

Institute of Technology (MIT) put it, "By the time that processed foods reach you, they may have been shipped and stored, trimmed, blanched, frozen, canned, condensed, dehydrated, pasteurized, sterilized, smoked, cured, milled, roasted, cooked, toasted or puffed. What's left of their composition after any combination of these tortures is then liable to be further stolen by heat, light, oxygen, oxalates, antivitamins, acidity, alkalinity, metal catalysts, enzymes, and irradiation."[13]

Take bread, for example. Whole wheat bread contains 24 known nutrients. White bread contains only 10 to 20 percent of these various vitamins and minerals—with the exception of "fortified" white bread, in which only *four* or *five* of the 24 depleted nutrients have been restored to acceptable levels!

This steady diet of such foods, lacking in nutrients or artificially "enriched" with only a few, leads inexorably to subclinical malnutrition. We aren't dying of pellagra or scurvy any more, but we're suffering from the subtler, yet still crippling effects of marginal nutrient deficiencies. Compared to people who lived hundreds or thousands of years ago, we eat a diet that is literally sickening.

Just how deadly is this diet? The evidence is clear from our health statistics. Our rate of type II diabetes, a "civilized" disease caused almost exclusively by bad diet, is astronomical, and rising annually. (Moreover, type II diabetes, once considered strictly a disease of people over 40, now strikes thousands of children—some of them as young as five or six.) Gallstones, strokes, heart disease, osteoporosis, and cancer plague us. So do obesity, constipation, hemorrhoids, and dental problems. Every one of these problems is caused, either in part or entirely, by a bad diet.

Our poor eating habits cause damage throughout our body, harming our hearts, our circulatory systems, our bones, our digestive systems, even our teeth. The brain is certainly not immune from this assault. Much of the bad behavior which plagues society today, and which is attributed to psychosociological causes, can be traced to dietary deficiencies. Correcting those deficiencies, rather than trying to treat them with often-futile counseling, psychotherapy, or self-esteem programs, can bring about much-needed improvement.

Recently, Bernard Gesch asked a group of violent prisoners to make a simple lifestyle change: adding a supplement of vitamins, minerals, and essential fatty acids to their diets. To judge the effects of this change, he gave half of the participants an active supplement, and the other half a placebo. Prisoners took the supplements or placebos for an average of 142 days.

The results were astonishing. Compared to the placebo group, prisoners taking the supplements committed an average of 26.3 percent fewer offenses. Gesch and his colleagues say, "The greatest reduction occurred for the most serious incidents, including violence," which dropped by an amazing 37 percent.

"The supplements just provided the vitamins, minerals and fatty acids found in a good diet which the inmates should get anyway," Gesch said. "Yet the improvement was huge." [14]

These results came as no surprise to Stephen Schoenthaler, because they duplicated his own findings almost exactly. Years earlier, Schoenthaler tested the effects of vitamin supplements on young adult offenders and found the supplements reduced the rate of serious rule violations by 38 percent. The data show, Schoenthaler says, that "violent behavior can be reduced significantly at a very low cost, making our schools and correctional institutions much safer." [15]

The brain is one of the first organs to suffer when you feed it junk food, because *every thought you have*, and *every behavior you initiate*, begins with *the food you eat*. Of course, if you're exceptionally healthy, you can live on doughnuts and cheeseburgers for a long time and still feel and act just fine. That's because your body stockpiles many nutrients. But nutritional deficiencies will eventually catch up with your brain, causing everything from "fuzzy" thinking to inappropriate aggression to depression and memory problems. To cite just a few examples:

- Iron deficiency anemia can cause problems ranging from learning impairment to conduct disorder and violence. [16]

- Low levels of vitamin B6 or folic acid correlate strongly with depression. In fact, as many as one third of people labeled as depressed have significant folic acid deficiencies.[17]

- Deficiencies of omega-3 fatty acids are tentatively linked to a host of learning and behavior problems ranging from depression to ADHD.[18]

- Children with chronic low B12 levels have problems with spatial skills, short-term memory, and fluid intelligence.[19]

- Zinc deficiency can cause memory and learning problems,[20] and it is linked to anorexia nervosa.[21]

Given the nutritional deficiencies of the typical American diet, it is no wonder that problems in behavior and logic are epidemic. Moreover, it's no surprise that, when we improve that diet, children's behavior often improves and their school performance often skyrockets.

Years ago, physicians Derrick Lonsdale and Raymond Shamberger evaluated the nutritional status of hostile, irritable, aggressive teens—teens who would, in this day and age, be labeled as "conduct disordered" and most likely put on mind-altering psychiatric drugs. But the teens didn't need drugs. The doctors found that a surprising number of them actually suffered from something you wouldn't expect to see in our modern society: vitamin B1 deficiency, causing symptoms severe enough to resemble subclinical beri-beri, and correctable with a good diet and supplements.[22] What were these children eating that could lead to a deficiency typically only seen in third-world countries? In most cases, French fries, sodas, candy bars, pizza—in short, a typical teen diet.

Additives add to the problem
Clearly, a diet lacking in nutrients can have catastrophic effects on mental health and IQ. For many dyslogical children and adults, however, the problem is not only too little good food, but too high an intake of semi-toxic stuff that isn't even food at all.

A good example is food dyes. Manufacturers now use *four times* as many of these dyes as they did in the 1950s,[23] putting them in everything from toothpastes to breakfast cereals and sodas. Kids get a heftier dose of food dyes than adults do, for two reasons. One is that children are smaller, so they receive a bigger dose per pound. The other is that the foods that youngsters like the most—cakes, sodas, and other junk foods—are the foods most likely to have artificial colorings.

Children's bodies aren't built to handle large amounts of such fake food, and it takes a toll on many of them. One study, for instance, found that a yellow food dye called tartrazine can cause behavior problems in children including "constant crying, tantrums, irritability, restlessness, and severe sleep disturbance," and that children sensitive to the food coloring become disruptive, easily distracted, uncontrollable, hyperactive, whiny, and/or "high as a kite" when they ingest the substance.[24]

Misled by the hype from the huge fake food conglomerates, doctors tend to scoff at the idea of a link between behavior and diet (and particularly food dyes and additives), but a report by the Center for Science in the Public Interest (CSPI) shows why they shouldn't. Researchers at CSPI reviewed 23 controlled studies of the effects of diet on hyperactivity, and determined that "17 of the 23 studies found evidence that some children's behavior significantly worsens after they consume artificial colors or certain foods, such as milk or wheat."[25] The most clear-cut evidence was for food dyes and additives.

One additive in particular that's currently raising serious questions is the artificial sweetener aspartame, now found in thousands of products. According to physician H.J. Roberts, "The FDA has received at least 6000 major complaints from 6000 consumers about aspartame products." Adverse reactions reported include seizures, headaches, ringing in the ears, irritability, and depression. Roberts adds, "Many observations suggest the ability of aspartame-containing products to cause or accelerate confusion, memory loss, altered behavior, intellectual deterioration, various allergies, and a host of neuropsychiatric, metabolic, ocular and developmental afflictions."[26]

Monosodium glutamate (MSG), a flavor enhancer you'll find in everything from cereals to chips and crackers, also may endanger a child's developing brain, in part because it mimics the action of the amino acid glutamate, a neurotransmitter. Physician Russell Blaylock, an expert on MSG's effects, explains, "Glutamate, as a neurotransmitter, is used by the brain only in very, very small concentrations—no more than 8 to 12 micrograms. When the concentration of this transmitter rises above this level the neurons begin to fire abnormally. At higher concentrations, the cells undergo a specialized process of cell death."[27] He notes that the blood-brain barrier, which under normal circumstances can prevent too much glutamate from entering the brain, is designed to handle small amounts of the substance—not a chronic overload caused by high daily doses.

Although the CSPI study found sugar to be less troublesome than most food additives, some studies show a strong correlation between a high-sugar diet and behavior problems. One interesting study, conducted on rats, approached the sugar/behavior issue from a different angle, investigating the possibility that sugar is actually addictive, in a manner similar to opium-like drugs—and that it is *withdrawal* from sugar, in the hours after a sugar binge, that makes children misbehave. The researchers reported that rats fed a high-sugar diet reacted to an opioid-antagonist drug in ways that suggested they had become "sugar dependent," and they suggest that "intermittent, excessive sugar intake might create dependency, as indicated by withdrawal signs."[28]

Sugar is harmful for still another reason: it crowds out good foods from the diet. Sugar consumption has risen rapidly during recent years, the current per capita consumption being more than 100 pounds per year. Children who fill up on that much sugar aren't hungry for the real foods that provide vitamins, minerals, protein, and other necessary nutrients.

A high-sugar and/or low-nutrient diet can also cause hypoglycemia, in which levels of blood sugar—the body's "fuel"—are too low to allow proper functioning of the brain and body. While many people laugh at the "Twinkie defense," there is much substance to the idea that hypoglycemia can lead to violence. Clinician Mary Jane Hungerford once noted that, in a large number of the cases she saw involving abusive spouses, violent periods were associated with abnormal blood glucose levels. These violent episodes often declined dramatically when excess sugar was removed and a healthful diet followed.[29]

Hidden hazards: when good food isn't good for the brain

Sometimes dyslogic-provoking substances aren't obvious culprits such as food dyes or sugar, but substances considered innocuous or even healthful—strawberries, milk, wheat flour, peanuts, etc.—to which a particular person is sensitive. Sensitivities occur when an individual's immune system mistakenly identifies one of these substances as an attacker and mounts a counter-attack, or when the body is unable to break down the substance correctly. If the substance is encountered frequently, the individual's body will be in a constant state of distress, with debilitating consequences—both physical and mental.

"In my general pediatric practice," the late William Crook said, "I've seen many, many pale, tired, nervous children with headache, abdominal pain, leg ache, and other systemic symptoms. Although I found some of these children to be suffering from such conditions as improper nutrition, chronic infection, or a psychosomatic disorder, in over 4000 of these youngsters...food allergy was the principal cause of their symptoms."

"Typical of the motor symptoms of some of these children is their restlessness and constant state of activity," he continued. "They fidget, twist, turn, grimace, jump, and jerk. They are often clumsy in using their voluntary muscles. They drop things, make noise, damage family possessions, and consequently bring on even more trouble for themselves. The sensory tension symptoms of irritability and inability to be pleased are perhaps the most common in these children. These personality traits, when exhibited repeatedly, gain for the child the reputation of being spoiled. Parents often wonder just where they have failed."[30]

Doris Rapp, M.D., has treated many children with food sensitivities. In her public talks, she likes to show videos of the dramatic effects such sensitivities can cause. Here is a transcript of a video of one child, Scott, who talks cooperatively with Dr. Rapp as he's given injections of a placebo substance. Next, he receives an injection containing an extract of a food to which he's sensitive. On the tape, he begins making a snorting sound common in allergic children, and starts rubbing his nose. The tone of his voice suddenly changes, becoming angry, and his conversation—previously friendly and pleasant—takes a frightening turn:

Mother: What do you want to do to us?
Scott: Blast this place to bits. Do away.
Doris Rapp: Do you want to draw me a picture? Draw me a picture.
Scott: No.
Doris Rapp: Come on.
Scott: No. I'll break that thing in half if you want me to. I'm going to break your neck.
Doris Rapp: Whose neck are you going to break?
Scott: All of yours. I'll break your neck in half.
Doris Rapp: Why? Why, Scott?
Scott: Because I don't like you. The people I don't like I break their necks and their fingers.
Doris Rapp: Why do you want to do such terrible things? Why do you want to hurt them? Why do you want to hurt people, Scott?
Scott: That's what I want to do, to kill.
Doris Rapp: Who do you want to kill?
Scott: Everyone. Everything and human beings. I hate them all… And it's worse when you're on an ugly planet like this.

What transformed Scott from a sweet, polite boy into a monster? A few simple, common foods that the rest of us can eat without any trouble—but which changed Scott, when he was exposed to them, from a delightful Dr. Jekyll into a terrifying Mr. Hyde.

For decades, Dr. Rapp treated children like Scott on a daily basis. In hundreds of cases, when she isolated food sensitivities and eliminated those foods from children's diets, their behavior problems—from school problems to life-threatening violence —vanished as well.[31]

In four decades of research, I've heard hundreds—perhaps, by now, thousands—of stories similar to the one above. I've met parents whose children become spacey, disoriented, or weepy if they eat certain additives. I've known children who exhibited every symptom of autism until their parents took them off milk or gluten-containing grains, and who then recovered almost completely—only to revert to their autistic behaviors when these foods were returned. And I've spoken with parents whose children behave perfectly normally, until they're exposed to food colorings—and then become violent, irrational, or even psychotic.

Despite such reports, most traditional allergists discount the idea that foods can cause mental problems. "It's amazing to me," psychiatrist Cathie-Ann Lippman commented. "I will say to my colleagues, 'Do you believe strawberries cause a rash?' and they will say, 'Sure.' Then I'll say, 'Do you think strawberries can cause a headache?' and they'll say, 'No.' And I'll say, 'Why not? If it can cause a problem in one organ, why not another organ?'"[32] And why not that most delicate of all organs—the brain?

I can understand these professionals' skepticism, however, because I too was skeptical when I first heard parents talking, decades ago, about how certain foods made their children behave aberrantly. But in the years since, I've witnessed many remarkable changes in children whose aberrant, violent, or self-injurious behavior was brought under control when offending foods were removed from their diets. I choose to believe the evidence. It is clear that food sensitivity can turn a happy, normal child into a monster—and that eliminating the troublesome food can often be more effective than all the Ritalin or Prozac in the world.

A friend of mine, hoping to help his learning disabled and behavior disordered young adult daughter, happened on the idea of giving her aspirin, on the theory that it might increase the blood flow to her brain. It was an interesting theory, but it backfired: a few hours after taking the aspirin, his daughter began behaving even more aberrantly than usual, and was belligerent, negative, and obnoxious. Curious, he repeated the experiment the next day, and then the next week, with the same results—only worse. "We just couldn't believe how in a few hours she could change into a real little bitch," he said. "The results certainly weren't what we had expected."

Knowing that aspirin was acetylsalicylic acid, my friend remembered that he'd heard allergist Ben Feingold, M.D., say that foods with natural salicylates, such as oranges, apples, plums, peaches, berries, tomatoes, apricots, cucumbers, and almonds, produced violent reactions in many children with food sensitivities. Testing these foods on his daughter, my friend found, indeed, that they could bring on, seemingly "out of the blue," an attack of anger, hostility, or other dyslogical behavior.

Diet and the unborn brain

The effects of a poor diet on older children, teens, and adults are crippling enough, but the effects of poor nutrition at the very beginnings of life are even more devastating. The brain of a fetus carried by a poorly nourished mother won't grow right, won't form the right neural connections, and won't ever function up to par. Similarly, the brain of an infant or toddler can't mature correctly if it's starved of the nutrients it needs. Thus, nutritional deficiencies before birth or early in childhood can cause learning and behavior problems that will haunt a child for life.

At greatest risk are the children of the 750,000 teenagers who give birth each year in the U.S. These adolescents, almost children themselves, are undertaking the most complex job on the planet: the construction of a new human life—and many of them are failing miserably, with tragic results for their children.

In addition to frequently smoking, drinking, and taking drugs (dangers I'll discuss in later chapters), thousands of these teenaged mothers eat the worst possible diet for their developing babies. Sodas, French fries, and potato chips are about as far from "brain food" as it's possible to get.

Even more critical, however, is what these mothers *don't* eat. Often, their diets are seriously deficient in vitamins, minerals, omega-3 fatty acids, and other nutrients needed to build a healthy baby. These deficiencies can have devastating effects on brain development, because during gestation a baby's brain grows thousands of neurons (nerve cells) each minute—and each of these cells has to migrate to the proper location and connect with the right combination of other neurons. Without a good supply of the right nutrients, brain development goes awry, causing subtle but crippling defects that can cause enduring, and perhaps permanent, brain damage. Harold Buttram, M.D., one of the nation's leading experts in environmental medicine, says:

> What's really bugged me throughout the years I've been in medicine is that 90 percent of interest and thrust is toward treatment, whereas prevention is relatively neglected. That's somewhat like ending the half of a football game behind 50 to nothing, and then hoping to catch up and win in the second half.[33]

A shortage of even one or two nutrients can be devastating to an unborn child's brain. For example, pregnant women who don't ingest enough zinc are twice as likely as other women to give birth to low-weight babies, and—if the deficiency occurs early in pregnancy—three times as likely to have a very preterm delivery.[34] That translates into thousands of infants born at high risk of learning disabilities, hyperactivity, and attention problems. A vitamin B6 deficiency *in utero* can stunt learning and memory by reducing the number of connections that form between a developing baby's brain cells, impairing myelination (the process in which brain cells form an insulating layer), and altering the brain's neurotransmitter systems.

A diet low in omega-3 fatty acids, and particularly DHA (docosahexaenoic acid), also can damage a child for a lifetime. These fatty acids, needed to form synaptic membranes, can't be produced by the body and must come from the diet—yet the foods and fats we commonly use don't contain omega-3s.

Can the damage done by a poor diet before birth, or in a child's early days, lead to conduct disorder, antisocial behavior, or criminality? Two large-scale studies say "yes." The first study analyzed data on thousands of Dutch men whose mothers were pregnant during the "Dutch Hunger Winter" of 1944–45, when the Nazis cut off food supplies to the Netherlands. The men whose mothers ate severely

restricted diets were much more likely, in adulthood, to exhibit "antisocial personality disorder"—a clinical way of saying that they grew up
to be aggressive, irresponsible, impulsive, remorseless, deceitful, and
prone to criminal acts.[35] What's more, earlier research found that the
survivors of this famine had an elevated rate of congenital defects of
the nervous system, a likely explanation for the cause of their criminal
behavior.[36] The second study of nearly 2000 children found that those
who showed signs of malnutrition at age 3 were more aggressive and
hyperactive at the age of 8, had more "externalizing behavior" (such as
aggression) at 11, and exhibited more conduct disorder and hyperactivity at 17 than well-fed children.[37]

Stunting our babies' brains

Before the days of pre-packaged formulas, almost all babies were
breastfed—if not by their own mothers, then by a wet nurse. Then
came "progress," in the form of commercial infant formulas, and
women weaned their babies early—or never breastfed them at all. In
spite of efforts over the last few decades to educate mothers about the
importance of breastfeeding, nearly half of American children
currently are bottle-fed rather than breastfed, and only 20 percent of
mothers breastfeed for more than four months.

This is an unhealthy trend, both for individual infants and for
society. "Infants deprived of breast milk are likely to have lower IQ,
lower educational achievement, and poorer social adjustment than
breastfed infants," says researcher James Anderson, who conducted a
review of 20 studies on the benefits of breastfeeding. Anderson found
that breast milk can increase babies' IQs an average of three to five
points[38]—a significant number, when you consider that there are only
30 points between average IQ (100) and retardation (70).

A more recent study, published in the *Journal of the American Medical
Association*, found a strong "dose effect" of breast feeding. Erik
Mortensen and colleagues evaluated data on the IQ scores of several
thousand adults who had been breastfed for varying lengths of time, or
not at all, during infancy. Their data revealed a steady climb in IQ as
the length of nursing increased, as shown below:

- average IQ of infants nursed less than one month: 99.4

- average IQ of infants nursed for two to three months: 101.7

- average IQ of infants nursed for four to six months: 102.3

- average IQ of infants nursed for seven to nine months: 106.0.

June Machover Reinisch, a member of the research team, said, "We are really quite certain that what we are seeing here is the effect of the duration of breastfeeding on an individual's intelligence…The evidence is growing that breastfeeding is among the most important lifelong benefits a mother can give to her child."[39]

Feeding an infant the formulas currently sold in grocery stores, conversely, can stunt a child's potential for life, because this formula often lacks key nutrients. For years, formulas lacked the essential fatty acids docosahexaenoic acid (DHA) and arachidonic acid (AA), which are just now beginning to be added to standard infant formula. The new addition of these fatty acids to infant formulas is a good move, but don't let that fool you into thinking that infant formula now provides complete nutrition for a developing baby's brain. In reality, formula is a poor substitute for the real thing.

"There is no substance that can come close to human milk," says nutrition expert Jennifer Taylor. "Infant formula is missing over 400 ingredients present in human milk, which cannot be duplicated by scientists in a laboratory." Yet, she notes, hospitals, pediatricians, and obstetricians routinely send new mothers home with free samples of formula.[40]

There is additional evidence that these formulas, currently used by millions of parents, are a less-than-perfect food for babies' developing brains. One group of researchers, comparing nine-year-old children who were breastfed as infants to children who were bottle-fed, reported, "Children who had been formula-fed were twice as likely to be diagnosed with a minor neurological dysfunction as those who had been breastfed."[41] Another group, studying pre-term babies, found that children given mother's milk in the early weeks of life had a significantly higher IQ at seven to eight years of age than the children who'd been bottle-fed. Even after the researchers controlled for mothers' education and social class, the preemies who were breastfed showed an 8.3-point IQ advantage.[42]

Infant formulas suffer in comparison to mother's milk not just because of the nutrients they lack, but also because of the potentially toxic substances they contain. Manganese, for instance, is present in tiny quantities in breast milk, but in vastly higher amounts—up to 200 times as much—in soy formulas. While the body needs some manganese, an excess is highly toxic to the brain, and especially to the developing brains of infants. Researcher Francis Crinella calculates that, by eight months of age, an infant given soy formula will absorb 1.1mg of manganese daily in excess of required amounts, and that about 8 percent of this excess is deposited in the basal ganglia, a brain region exquisitely vulnerable to manganese toxicity.[43]

Says Stanley Van Den Noort, a neurology professor and former Dean of the University of California Irvine College of Medicine, "I think the data…are convincing that manganese is a neurotoxin. Newborn infants exposed to high levels of manganese may be predisposed to neurological problems. We should exercise strong caution in the use of soy-based formula around the world."[44]

In addition to their high manganese content, soy formulas are rich in plant-based estrogens that can alter the hormone levels of developing male and female infants—possibly with disastrous consequences. Carol Simontacchi, a clinical nutritionist and author of *The Crazy Makers*, an exposé of the deleterious effects of processed foods on American children's physical and mental health, notes:

> Boys on soy-based formulas not only are manufacturing large amounts of testosterone but also are ingesting huge amounts of estrogen. Receiving these confusing hormonal messages can wreak havoc with their emotionality. Many women know that imbalances in estrogen cause the quintessential menopause symptoms of depression, hostility, and aggressiveness. What does the excess estrogen do to little boys?

We have no idea, but Simontacchi points out that, in rodents, excessive estrogen during the fetal period can lead to aggression, aberrant behavior, and hyperactivity, in addition to greatly elevating the risk for cancer.[45]

We know too little about other possible consequences of feeding our infants artificial milk from cans or packages. What we do know, without a doubt, however, is that breast milk—unlike artificial formulas—is designed to fill an infant's needs (except for the possibility of contamination with mercury—see Chapter 6). The breast milk of a woman eating a healthful diet contains all of the nutrients her baby's brain needs, from omega-3 fatty acids to vitamins and minerals, as well as disease-fighting antibodies and a perfect balance of protein, carbohydrates, and fats. Doctors who fail to explain this to new mothers, and who hand out formula samples instead of encouraging mothers to breastfeed, are actively contributing to America's epidemic of dyslogical brains.

Food for thought

As a parent who raised three children, I know that it isn't always easy to feed our children right. In the early years, it can be tough for a busy working mother to juggle a career and breastfeeding, making it tempting to reach for a can of formula instead. Later, as children are indoctrinated by TV commercials and enticed by colorful junk-food packages at the store, feeding a youngster can become a test of wills.

A child who loves orange-colored soda but reacts violently to food colorings is likely to cry, whine, or even kick and scream when he doesn't get his favorite pop any more. A child accustomed to sugar-coated cereals may make a parent's life miserable for weeks when those cereals are absent from his breakfast table. (Many children appear to be "addicted" to the foods that harm them the most.) And a child who's unaccustomed to a simple, unprocessed diet of healthful fruits, vegetables, grains, and other healthy foods is likely to rebel, particularly at first.

But this is a battle well worth fighting, especially for parents whose children's problems could otherwise lead to academic failure, trouble with the law, and constant crises and anguish. And it is a battle that needs to be fought by our schools and our prisons as well.

Carol Simontacchi, whose work I cited earlier, describes the effects that dietary intervention can have on even the most troubled children, using the case of a young man released from jail. When Simontacchi first evaluated Jake, his test scores for tension, depression, anger, hostility, and confusion were nearly off the charts. After just a few weeks of eating a healthful diet and taking supplements, he tested in the normal range. "He may need to work on anger management or life skills with a counselor," Simontacchi says, "but Jake is, for the first time in his life, in control of his brain and his emotions."[46]

There are millions of Jakes in America's jails and prisons, and millions more struggling to learn school subjects that they can't understand because their brains are deprived of the nutrients they need, and are overloaded with artificial additives and colorings that their bodies can't handle. These children and adults will be a threat to themselves, and a threat and a burden to society as a whole, as long as we continue to ignore the simple fact that a brain starving for the nutrients it needs, and laden with artificial chemicals that it can't handle, is a dangerous brain.

Notes

1   For an in-depth look at the biochemical diversity of human beings, I highly recommend Williams, R. (1998) *Biochemical Individuality.* New York: McGraw-Hill.

2   Cited by Beasley, J. (1991) in *The Betrayal of Health.* New York: Times Books, p.58.

3   "Impact of Healthy Foods on Learning and Behavior: Five Year Study." DVD, published by Natural Ovens Bakery, Inc., P.O. Box 730, Manitowoc, WI 54221, October 2004.

4   Schoenthaler, S. (1986) "The impact of a low food additive and sucrose diet on academic performance in 803 New York City public schools." *International Journal of Biosocial Research 8*, 2, 185–95.

5   Benton, D. and Roberts, G. (1988) "Effect of vitamin and mineral supplementation on intelligence of a sample of schoolchildren." *The Lancet*, I, 140–3.

6   Coleman, M., Steinberg, G., Tippett, J., Bhagavan, H.N., Coursin, D.B., Gross, M., Lewis, C. and DeVeau, L. (1979) "A preliminary study of the effect of pyridoxine administration in a subgroup of hyperkinetic children: A double-blind crossover comparison with methylphenidate." *Biological Psychiatry 14*, 5, 741–51.

7   Harding, K.L., Judah, R.D. and Gant, C. (2003) "Outcome-based comparison of Ritalin versus food-supplement treated children with ADHD." *Alternative Medicine Review 8*, 3, 319–30.

8   Mousain-Bosc, M., Roche, M., Polge, A., Pradai-Prat, D., Rapin, J. and Bali, J.P. (2006) "Improvement of neurobehavioral disorders in children supplemented

with magnesium-vitamin B6. I. Attention deficit hyperactivity disorder." *Magnesium Research 19*, 1, 46–52.

9 Richardson, A.J. and Montgomery, P. (2005) "The Oxford–Durham Study: A randomized controlled trial of dietary supplementation with fatty acids in children with developmental coordination disorder." *Pediatrics 115*, 5, 1360–6.

10 "U.S. children failing to meet national dietary recommendations," *Doctor's Guide*, September 1997.

11 "Report card on the diet quality of children ages 2 to 9." US Department of Agriculture, Center for Nutrition Quality and Promotion, September 2001. Available at www.cnp.usda.gov/publications/NutritionInsights/Insight25.pdf (accessed 27 September 2007).

12 Beasley, J. (1991) *The Betrayal of Health*. New York: Times Books, p.63.

13 Harris, R.S. cited in E. Cheraskin, W.M. Ringsdorf and E. Sisley (1983) *The Vitamin C Connection*. New York: Harper & Row, p.29.

14 Gesch, C.B., Hammond, S.M., Hampson, S.E., Eves, A. and Crowder, J.M. (2002) "Influence of supplementary vitamins, minerals and essential fatty acids on the antisocial behaviour of young adult prisoners: Randomized, placebo-controlled trial." *British Journal of Psychiatry 181*, 22–8.

15 Shoenthaler's research cited in "Professor Schoenthaler's nutrition research reveals link between vitamin supplements and reduced violent behavior," press release, California State University, July 3, 2002.

16 Bruner, A.B., Joffe, A., Duggan, A.K., Casella, J.F. and Brandt, J. (1996) "Randomised study of cognitive effects of iron supplementation in non-anaemic iron-deficient adolescent girls." *Lancet 348*, 9033, 992–6; and Tu, J.B., Shafey, H. and VanDewetering, C. (1994) "Iron deficiency in two adolescents with conduct, dysthymic and movement disorders." *Canadian Journal of Psychiatry 39*, 6, 371–5.

17 Alpert, J.E. and Fava, M. (1997) "Nutrition and depression: The role of folate." *Nutrition Review 55*, 5, 145–9.

18 McNamara, R.K. and Carlson, S.E. (2006) "Role of omega-3 fatty acids in brain development and function: Potential implications for the pathogenesis and prevention of psychopathology." *Prostaglandins, Leukotrienes, and Essential Fatty Acids 75*, 4–5, 329–49.

19 Louwman, M.W., van Dusseldorp, M., van de Vijver, F.J., Thomas, C.M., Schneede, J., Ueland, P.M., Refsum, H. and van Staveren, W.A. (2000) "Signs of impaired cognitive function in adolescents with marginal cobalamin status." *American Journal of Clinical Nutrition 72*, 3, 762–9.

20 Halas, E.S., Eberhardt, M.J., Diers, M.A. and Sandstead, H.H. (1983) "Learning and memory impairment in adult rats due to severe zinc deficiency during lactation." *Physiology and Behavior 30*, 3, 371–81.

21 Tannhauser, P.P. (2002) "Anorexia nervosa: A multifactorial disease of nutritional origin?" *International Journal of Adolescent Medicine and Health 14*, 3, 185–91.

22 Lonsdale, D. and Shamberger, R.J. (1980) "Red cell transketolase as an indicator of nutritional deficiency." *American Journal of Clinical Nutrition 33*, 205–11.

23 Jacobson, M.F. and Schardt, D. (1999) *Diet, ADHD and Behavior: A Quarter-Century Review.* Washington, DC: Center for Science in the Public Interest.

24 Rowe, K.S. and Rowe, K.J. (1994) "Synthetic food coloring and behavior: A dose response effect in a double-blind, placebo-controlled, repeated-measures study." *Journal of Pediatrics 125*, 5, 691–8.

25 Jacobson, M.F. and Schardt, D. (1999) *Diet, ADHD, and Behavior: A Quarter-Century Review.* Washington, DC: Center for Science on the Public Interest.

26 Nutrition for Optimal Health Association, Inc. (1993) "Aspartame (NutraSweet.)" *NOHA News 18*, 1.

27 Blaylock, R.L. "Excitotoxins – Not Just Another Scare." Available at www.nisbett.com/nutrition/excitotoxins01.htm (accessed 8 October 2007).

28 Colantuoni, C., Rada, P., McCarthy, J., Patten, C., Avena, N.M., Chadeayne, A. and Hoebel, B.G. (2002) "Evidence that intermittent, excessive sugar intake causes endogenous opioid dependence." *Obesity Research 10*, 6, 478–88.

29 Schauss, A.G. (1982) "Effects of environmental and nutritional factors on potential and actual batterers." In M. Roy (ed.) (1982) *The Abusive Partner: An Analysis of Domestic Battering.* New York: Van Nostrand Reinhold.

30 Crook, W.G. (1975) "Food allergy – the great masquerader." *Pediatric Clinics of North America 22*, 1, 227.

31 For more information about Doris Rapp's work, see her books including *Is This Your Child's World?* New York: Bantam, 1996, and *Is This Your Child?* New York: William Morrow & Company, Inc., 1991. For more information about the work of the late William Crook, see his books including *Tracking Down Hidden Food Allergy.* New York: McGraw-Hill, 1980.

32 Gelman, D., King, P., Hager, M., Raine, G. and Pratt, J. (1985) "The food–mood link." *Newsweek*, October 14.

33 Personal communication.

34 Scholl, T.O., Hediger, M.L., Schall, J.I., Fischer, R.L. and Khoo, C.S. (1993) "Low zinc intake during pregnancy: Its association with preterm and very preterm delivery." *American Journal of Epidemiology 137*, 10, 1115–24.

35 Neugebauer, R., Hoek, H.W. and Susser, E. (1999) "Prenatal exposure to wartime famine and development of antisocial personality disorder in early adulthood." *Journal of the American Medical Association 282*, 5, 455–62.

36 Beasley, J. (1991) *The Betrayal of Health.* New York: Times Books.

37 Liu, J., Raine, A., Venables, P.H. and Mednick, S.A. (2004) "Malnutrition at age 3 years and externalizing behavior problems at ages 8, 11 and 17 years." *American Journal of Psychiatry 161*, 11, 2005–13.

38 Quote is from "Breastfeeding linked to higher IQ." *Reuters*, September 22, 1999.

39 Mortensen, E.L., Michaelsen, K.F., Sanders, S.A. and Reinisch, J.M. (2002) "The association between duration of breastfeeding and adult intelligence." *Journal of the American Medical Association 287*, 18, 2365–71; and Kaufman, M. (2002) "Breastfeeding linked to IQ gain." *Washington Post*, May 8, p.A01.

40 Taylor, J. "North American culture: Undermining breastfeeding." Available at www.obgyn.net (accessed 8 October 2007).

41 Lanting, C.I., Fidler, V., Huisman, M., Touwen, B.C.L. and Boersma, E.R. (1994) "Neurological differences between 9-year-old children fed breastmilk or formula-milk as babies." *The Lancet 344*, 8933, 1319–22.

42 Lucas, A., Morley, R., Cole, T.J., Lister, G. and Leeson-Payne, C. (1992) "Breast milk and subsequent intelligence quotient in children born preterm." *The Lancet 339*, 8788, 261–4.

43 Goodman, D. (2001) "How safe is soy infant formula?" Insight on the News, 25 June.

44 Goodman, D., n.d. "Manganese Madness." Available at www.westonaprice.org/soy/manganese.html (accessed 27 September 2007).

45 Simontacchi, C. (2000) *The Crazy Makers*. New York: Tarcher/Putnam, p.71.

46 Ibid. p.72.

CHAPTER 6

The Contaminated Brain: How our Toxic Environment Affects our Children's Thinking

"Evil may be something no more sinister than a matter of loose connections. The devil may be the term for an accumulation of cerebral wounds."

—Anne Moir and David Jessel, *A Mind to Crime*[1]

Inside an unborn baby's brain, amazing things happen. Following the commands of hormones and neurotransmitters, cells migrate to their assigned locations. Between these neurons, billions of branching connections sprout. Cells begin to form insulating myelin sheaths, so they can transmit accurate messages instantaneously. Moment by moment, the brain grows and changes.

After birth, development continues. New cell connections form constantly, while the brain ruthlessly prunes away those it no longer needs, and the process of myelinization accelerates. Working twice as hard as an adult brain, the child's brain ceaselessly molds itself into an astonishingly efficient machine for learning, thinking, and feeling.

This is delicate work, predicated on perfect chemistry and timing. If all goes well, a miracle—a fully functioning human brain—occurs. Too few cells in one area, too many in another, a defect in myelinization, an excess or dearth of connections, and the consequences can be devastating: low intelligence, malfunctions in the frontal lobes that control reason and logic, altered development of regions that control learning or impulse control, even impairment of the systems that make us human by allowing us to love or fear or feel empathy.

Picture this microscopic world of precisely timed and exquisitely balanced chemical reactions, far too complex for the most powerful computers to duplicate. Now, picture what happens if you explode a grenade—in the form of alcohol, tobacco, cocaine, pesticides, mercury, lead, or other toxins—in this fragile internal ecosystem.

George Michael Hodges grew up in the 1950s and 1960s, in a poor Appalachian neighborhood next to the Kanawha River in West Virginia. The son of a chronically unemployed alcoholic, Hodges scrounged for toys, clothing, and even partly eaten food from the town's grossly polluted garbage dump. His family caught fish from the Kanawha, a river that was then so toxic as a result of chemical dumping that its fish often died or suffered from bizarre deformities. The Hodges children swam in water contaminated with cyanide, manganese, lead, mercury, and cadmium.

When the Hodges children reached school age, George was diagnosed with a verbal learning disability, and his brother Randy was diagnosed with attention deficit hyperactivity disorder. Both also suffered head injuries from beatings inflicted by their father, a convicted sex criminal. George's speech problems and academic difficulties made him the butt of teasing and bullying at school, where he had only one friend, a mentally retarded boy.

George Michael Hodges and Betty Ricks never met when George was growing up. Their lives first intersected many years later in 1986, when Hodges—then 29 years old—exposed himself to Ricks. She filed charges, insisting that he be prosecuted. On a January morning in 1987, Betty Ricks stepped out of her car, headed for the store where she worked. Seconds later, she lay dead, shot by Hodges. A jury convicted Hodges in 1989, and he remains on Death Row today.

George Michael Hodges committed a cold-blooded and irrational murder—one that stole a life and left Betty Ricks' family grieving. It is accurate to say that he committed an act of pure, senseless evil. It may be fair to say, too, that his behavior stemmed in part from his impoverished childhood, and his abusive upbringing—as well as his poor diet, and a genetic burden from a mentally disturbed father.

But we can't know what drove George Michael Hodges without factoring in the chemical sea in which he grew up: a sea of cyanide, manganese, lead, mercury, and cadmium, each one a toxin capable of crippling and destroying brain cells. These toxins entered Hodges' body in every glass of water he drank, every fish he ate from the Kanawha River, every half-eaten box of cereal he scrounged from the toxic dump, and every breath he took, from the day he was born until the day he was arrested. A toxicologist testified that Hodges' neighborhood was a "cesspool," containing toxins sufficient to cause neurological deficits, low IQ, and behavior aberrations.[2]

A lab animal raised in an environment contaminated by these toxins would almost undoubtedly exhibit behavioral and cognitive anomalies, up to and including bizarre sexual behavior and homicidal rages; should it surprise us that a human being reacts in much the same way? It is not remarkable in the least that Hodges, his brother, and his father were severely dysfunctional. It would be remarkable if they weren't.

George Michael Hodges is only one of many criminals with clearly toxic brains. The most famous, perhaps, is James Huberty, who walked into a McDonald's in San Ysidro, California, in 1984 and shot 21 people dead before police killed him. When the medical examiner autopsied Huberty's body, he found an astonishingly high level of cadmium, a neurotoxic heavy metal. The examiner called William

Walsh, an authority on metal poisoning and behavior, to ask: "If Huberty had this much cadmium in his body, why wasn't he dead?"[3]

Pollution, however, doesn't turn most of its victims into killers. Instead, it cripples them more insidiously, lowering their IQs and stunting their brain development just enough to leave them somewhat less intelligent, somewhat less socially capable, or somewhat less empathetic to their fellow human beings. One good example of this invisible damage comes from research by Elizabeth Guillette, who studied two groups of Yaqui Indian children living in Mexico. One group lived in the lowlands, which are sprayed heavily with pesticides. The other lived in the nearly pesticide-free foothills. Otherwise, the two groups of children were very much alike, both genetically and culturally. Guillette and her colleagues expected to detect some subtle differences between the pesticide-exposed and non-exposed children. What they found, however, horrified them.

The pesticide-exposed children could barely draw, producing primitive scribbles rather than the well-defined stick figures that the unexposed children drew easily. They couldn't remember a statement accurately after 30 minutes. They were violent, hitting their brothers and sisters, and acting out against their parents. "Overall," Guillette and her colleagues say, "disruptive behavior was the norm."[4] It's likely that few of these children will grow up to be killers; but it's equally likely that they will suffer, and make others around them suffer, as a result of the damage done to their brains by years of chemical exposure.

Toxic overload

The pesticides that Guillette studied, and the heavy metals that contaminated the brains of James Huberty and George Michael Hodges, are only a few of the thousands of chemicals we spray, pour, sprinkle, paint, and flush into our environment. Every day we expose our children to poisons their bodies were never designed to handle, from fertilizers and weed sprays to solvents and bathroom cleansers. More than eight million metric tons of synthetic chemicals are produced each year, and a third of these chemicals have *known* toxic properties. It's certain that many of the others cause serious harm in ways we haven't yet discovered. And it's also certain that many chemicals that are harmless when used alone can become toxic when mixed with other chemicals in our air, water, and soil.

While we're all at risk for brain impairment from toxins, young children suffer far more from exposure than adults. Because of their smaller size, they consume proportionately more toxins. Babies and young children also spend much of their time crawling on the floor or ground, where concentrations of pollutants are highest. And their liver and kidney functions are not yet fully developed, so young children cannot detoxify or eliminate dangerous substances as effectively as adults.

Even older children, however, live in a toxic world. Kids spend more time playing in the street or on the grass than adults, increasing their exposure to everything from heavy metals to herbicides and pesticides. They also have poorer hygiene than most grown-ups, and what gets on their hands—from gasoline to bug spray to furniture polish—often gets into their mouths. Well into the teenage years, their brains are still changing dramatically, and still highly vulnerable to the brain-stunting effects of toxins, especially when drugs or alcohol are added to the mix.

In some cases, the damage that this toxic burden does to children's brains is all too obvious. Children bathed in ethanol before birth by their alcoholic mothers, for instance, often have heartbreaking physical and mental defects. Children poisoned by huge amounts of methyl mercury are horribly crippled, in both body and mind. Teenagers who chronically sniff glue or use the "street drug" ecstasy can suffer permanent brain damage leading to learning disabilities or movement disorders. But in the vast majority of cases, the destruction is far more subtle, and easier to overlook.

Even subtle damage, however, can be enough to ruin a child's life. It can be the difference between a child who graduates with honors, and a child who struggles to learn basic skills. It can change a happy child into a troubled, depressed, or even suicidal individual. And it can make a child into a troublemaker, a criminal, or a killer.

One group of researchers followed 20 children treated for mild lead poisoning, evaluating them several years after treatment. Nineteen

*were found to be suffering from behavioral and learning problems,
even though all had been considered "cured" when discharged from
the hospital. Many of the children were hyperactive, or prone to
impulsive and violent acts, and three had been expelled from
school—one for setting fires, one for dancing on the desks, and the
third for sticking a fork into another child's face.[5]*

*"The education community has really not understood the
dimensions of [lead toxicity] because we don't see kids falling over
and dying of lead poisoning in the classroom," Bailus Walker,
former commissioner of public health in Massachusetts, once
commented. "But there's a very large number of kids who find it
difficult to do analytical work or [even] line up in the cafeteria
because their brains are laden with lead."[6]*

Given a heavy enough load of mind-altering chemicals, any child will
succumb to "toxic dyslogic," but even lower levels of chemicals and
heavy metals can devastate the brain, particularly when they combine
in unexpected ways. One study, for instance, found that, when pesticides, herbicides, and fertilizers combine in our groundwater, their
synergistic effects on the brain and immune system are worse than for
each chemical alone. Mixed together, the chemicals had dramatic
effects on test animals' thyroid function (which can affect intelligence,
learning, and irritability or aggression), even at levels considered safe
for the individual chemicals.[7]

Children's bodies now contain thousands of foreign substances,
from plastics and flame retardants to fertilizers and carpet cleaners,
making them, in effect, living "cocktails" of alien chemicals and metals.
No doctor or scientist can predict how these substances will react with
each other, or how these interactions will affect the brains of generations of human guinea pigs. But given our rising rates of learning disabilities, childhood depression, and other mental disorders, the
answers—if we are ever brave enough to seek them—are likely to be
unsettling.

Even more unsettling is the recent finding that toxic exposures can
harm not just an exposed individual, but the person's children and

grandchildren as well. We're discovering that toxic exposure can cause "epigenetic" effects, which are changes in gene function that occur in the absence of structural changes in DNA sequencing, and which can be inherited. For example, one study found that when pregnant rats were exposed to a high dose of a particular pesticide, 90 percent of the male offspring in the next four generations had reproductive problems. Other research shows that epigenetic alterations can cause multi-generational behavior changes as well.[8]

A recent study by the Environmental Working Group found that newborn babies have an average of 200 industrial chemicals and pollutants in their bodies. Among them: pesticides, consumer product ingredients, and wastes from burning garbage, coal, and gasoline. In all, the researchers detected 287 chemicals in umbilical cord blood samples. Of these, they say, "We know that 180 cause cancer in humans or animals, 217 are toxic to the brain and nervous system, and 208 cause birth defects or abnormal development in animal tests."[9]

The top threats to our children's brains

While we know far too little about the chemical stew in which our children live, we do know enough about many toxins to brand them as major players in the dyslogic epidemic. These toxins are particularly dangerous for two reasons: they have devastating effects on neurons, and they're so widespread that millions of children are at risk of high exposure. They include the following.

Endocrine disruptors

Chemicals called "endocrine disruptors" latch onto the same cell receptors as estrogen or other endocrine hormones. When they do this, they mimic or block normal hormones, throwing off the body's intricate chemical balance. Endocrine disruptors are linked to cancer, birth defects, reproductive problems, and brain changes that may alter thinking and behavior.

While researchers are just now studying the developmental effects of several widely used endocrine disruptors—among them, bisphenol

A and phthalates, both used in plastics—other forms of these chemicals have been investigated more thoroughly, and the results aren't encouraging.

One class of endocrine disruptors that's been investigated for years is PCBs, now banned but still pervasive in the environment. In 1996, Joseph and Sandra Jacobson reported that children exposed to high doses of PCBs during prenatal development have lowered intelligence, increasing their risk for school failure.[10] Joseph Jacobson commented to *Science News*:

> I thought that once they reached a structured school environment, whatever minor handicaps [the children with high PCB exposures] had would be overcome. So I was quite surprised to find that, if anything, the effects were stronger and clearer at age 11 than they had been at age 4.[11]

Unfortunately, PCBs find their way even into the healthiest of baby foods, breast milk. One study followed 171 mothers and their healthy babies, testing the babies at four different ages. The researchers found that babies whose mothers had the highest concentrations of PCBs in their breast milk had significantly lower mental and motor development scores at 30 months and beyond.[12]

Pesticides

Almost every American household contains pest strips, bug bombs, flea collars, bait boxes, pesticide sprays and powders, and pesticide-containing pet shampoos, as well as extremely toxic herbicides. Moreover, many homeowners dilute concentrated pesticides or herbicides far less than labels recommend, thereby exposing their children to huge doses. Children also encounter pesticides and herbicides on their soccer fields, in their food, in termite treated buildings, and in their drinking water.

The casual manner in which we use these chemicals leads us to believe that they're safe. However, many are endocrine disruptors (see previous section) and most are toxic to the developing nervous system. Organophosphate pesticides, for instance, are close cousins to the nerve gases invented by German scientists for use in World War II. These chemicals work by interfering with the breakdown of the messenger chemical acetylcholine, causing toxic levels to accumulate. In insects, this causes death due to catastrophic failure of the nervous system. In an unborn child, repeated exposure can cause altered brain development[13]—and after birth, chronic exposure can cause anxiety, confusion, seizures, stupor, or even outright psychosis.[14]

Alcohol

For decades, doctors told pregnant women, "Have a drink or two at night—it'll relax you." We now know, however, that even moderate drinking can cause a crippling syndrome called Fetal Alcohol Effects (FAE), and that heavy drinking during pregnancy can cause a child to be born with Fetal Alcohol Syndrome (FAS), a tragic form of mental retardation.

Unfortunately, many pregnant women *don't* know that there may be *no safe amount of alcohol* for unborn children. Recently, researchers collected data on more than 500 women who had received prenatal care at an urban clinic. When the women's children were six to seven years of age, the researchers evaluated their behavior. "Significantly," the researchers say, "children with low levels of prenatal alcohol exposure—equivalent to an average of one cocktail per week across pregnancy—were three times as likely to have delinquent behavior scores in the clinical range," even when the researchers controlled for other social and biological factors.[15]

This doesn't mean, of course, that every woman who drinks during pregnancy will have a child with FAS or FAE. The more a woman drinks, however, the greater her risk will be of giving birth to a brain-damaged child. The cost of full-blown FAS is astronomical, with each severely affected child costing society 2 million dollars over a lifetime. But FAE, while considered less serious, can often lead to even greater problems. That's because individuals with FAE often function at a high enough level to live independently, yet most lack the self-control and judgment needed to be responsible adults. As a result, it's estimated that of people with Fetal Alcohol Effects:

- 68 percent will experience some sort of trouble with legal authorities

- 95 percent will have mental health problems

- 52 percent will exhibit inappropriate sexual behavior

- 55 percent will be confined at some point in a prison, mental institution, or drug/alcohol treatment center.[16]

One September day in Elgin, Arizona, a 15-year-old named Jonathan McMullen shot his adoptive mother to death. He loved his mother, but he'd been talked into committing the crime by a 12-year-old friend, who convinced Jonathan to shoot his family members so that the two boys could take the family car and have fun. Jonathan, who has Fetal Alcohol Syndrome, also wounded his father and brother in the attack.

Now facing murder charges, Jonathan says he wishes he could give all of his allowance money to get his mother back. He also wants to know when he can come home. Although two psychiatrists testified that Jonathan's alcohol-caused brain damage left him incapable of controlling his behavior, a judge ruled him competent to stand trial as an adult.

Tobacco

Once thought to be relatively harmless to the developing fetus, the chemicals contained in tobacco smoke are proving to have powerful behavior-altering effects. More than a dozen studies show very strong links between maternal smoking during pregnancy and behavior problems or delinquency in offspring. For instance, David Fergusson and colleagues found that children whose mothers smoked one or more packs of cigarettes per day during pregnancy had twice as many conduct disorder symptoms as children born to mothers who did not smoke during pregnancy.[17]

The studies conducted to date link pregnant women's smoking to an increased risk in their offspring for hyperactivity, poor impulse control, oppositional behavior, aggression, psychiatric problems, substance abuse, reduced intelligence, delinquency, and adult criminality. Patricia Brennan and her colleagues, whose research detected a powerful connection between maternal smoking and criminality and psychiatric illness in girls, note that, while most children whose mothers smoke during pregnancy do not become criminals or substance abusers, "our study suggests that prenatal smoking cessation programs may have the potential to reduce not only negative physical health outcomes, but also negative behavioral health outcomes, in future generations of children."[18]

Lead

Despite our ban on lead-laden gasoline and paints, current environmental lead levels are five hundred times higher than the natural levels found in centuries-old glacial ice.[19] "Even in the superficially clean setting of the suburbs," toxicologist Bernard Weiss notes, "children exhibit body burdens of lead many times higher than those revealed by human skeletons in eras before the development of mining and smelting."[20]

How much lead is dangerous? A recent study by Bruce Lanphear[21] found that even at five micrograms per deciliter, a level only half as high as government standards allow, children show IQ deficits. Herbert Needleman and colleagues, studying children without overt lead toxicity, found that those with the highest lead levels had a sevenfold increase in failure to graduate from high school, and a significantly higher risk of having reading disabilities.[22]

More recently, Needleman reported that, even in children without overt lead toxicity, elevated lead levels are strongly associated with aggression, antisocial behavior, and delinquency. Overall, he found, bone lead levels are twice as high in teenage delinquents as in non-delinquent high-school students.[23] "If [our] findings are found to extend to the population of U.S. children," he says, "the contribution of lead to delinquent behavior would be substantial."[24]

Many children may be at high risk for lead-induced brain dysfunction because of the water they drink. Dartmouth professors Roger Masters and Myron Coplan have studied lead toxicity in American communities, and they report, "Wherever there is lead pollution in the environment, the use of silicofluorides in water treatment increases lead uptake in the body and brain." The researchers say that many communities that once fluoridated their water with sodium fluoride, on which safety data were based, now use silicofluorides that can break down incompletely and make water more acidic, causing more lead to leach from pipes. In addition, they believe that silicofluoride residues may help transport lead into the blood from the gastrointestinal tract.[25]

Mercury

The mind-altering effects of this highly toxic metal are well known; in fact, the "Mad Hatter" in *Alice in Wonderland* is based on symptoms seen in workers who made felt hats in Lewis Carroll's time. The felt hat makers, who were exposed to mercury, frequently became irritable and restless, and developed tremors and speech abnormalities.

While virtually no one gets the "hatter's shakes" anymore, everyone is at risk for mercury toxicity. Fossil-fueled power plants spew tons of mercury into the atmosphere each year, while both fresh-water and salt-water fish often contain dangerously high levels of mercury. As a result, according to the Environmental Protection Agency, one in six pregnant women now has mercury levels high enough to harm the brain development of a fetus.[26] Worse yet, until recently, children received large doses of mercury through another route: doctors injected it directly into their veins in the form of mercury-containing vaccines. Increasing evidence, which I'll detail in Chapter 7, links this exposure to hyperactivity, learning disorders, and autism.

Cadmium

Earlier, I noted that James Huberty, who killed 21 people at a McDonald's, had almost impossibly high levels of this toxic metal in his body, apparently as a result of his job as a welder. High levels of cadmium are strongly linked to violent or aberrant behavior; in fact, one theory about the artist Vincent Van Gogh is that he cut off his ear because he was mentally ill as a result of licking cadmium-laced paintbrushes. Even moderately elevated levels of cadmium can cause "mental meltdown" in vulnerable brains.

Robert O. Pihl and his colleagues, analyzing hair samples from learning disabled and non-disabled students, reported that cadmium was the mineral most closely associated with learning problems.[27] In addition, they found that violent criminals have higher levels of both lead and cadmium than do their nonviolent counterparts.[28] More recently, researcher Jack Nation has found that prenatal exposure to cadmium and/or lead appears to increase the tolerance for cocaine and alcohol, in effect "programming" children to be more susceptible to later substance abuse.[29]

Manganese

In the last chapter, I provided evidence that our current epidemic of dyslogic may stem, in part, from soy infant formulas, which contain large amounts of manganese. As a result of ingesting these formulas, young children—whose brains appear to be much more sensitive to manganese than the brains of adults—are exposed to levels of manganese far above normal, particularly if they live near landfills or their parents work in industries involving manganese exposure.

Manganese is required by our brains and bodies in small amounts. In large amounts, however, it's a powerful neurotoxin; in fact, before more stringent safety rules went into effect, manganese miners often developed a disorder called "manganese madness," leading to psychosis, motor problems, and eventually death.

There's substantial evidence linking elevated manganese exposure to dyslogic. One group of researchers, for instance, found significantly elevated levels of manganese in the head hair of the violent adult male criminals they studied.[30] Elevated hair manganese levels are also seen in hyperactive children, and rats become hyperactive and fight more often when chronically exposed to excess levels of manganese.[31]

These toxins are among the worst of the worst, particularly when it comes to brain dysfunction. But our children encounter thousands of additional chemicals, including the solvents we use in our garages, the cleansers we use in our kitchens, laundry rooms, and bathrooms, the fire retardants in bedding, and the formaldehyde in our furniture and carpets. While these toxins may cause cancer or migraines or asthma in many millions of children, millions of others express their illness in behavioral ways: a "Jekyll and Hyde" personality, uncontrollable silliness, irritability, hostility, aggression, vulgar language, depression, hitting, biting, punching, spitting, and kicking. Many have difficulty writing, learning, or memorizing. And many are the children scolded for "spacing out" or daydreaming in class, when in reality their chemical-laden brains are no more capable of concentrating than is the brain of a drunk after a six-Martini binge.

Sadly, few disruptive, learning disabled, depressed, or delinquent children ever see the few doctors who are really aware of the damage that toxic chemicals can do to vulnerable brains. Instead, many wind up being referred to psychologists or "anger control counselors" who can't fix brain dysfunction. Worse, millions wind up in the offices of doctors who prescribe Ritalin, Adderall, or antidepressants or antipsychotics—thus adding even more toxic foreign substances to these children's already dysfunctional brains.

To help these children, we need to stop wasting precious time with largely ineffective talk therapy, or further polluting their brains with toxic drugs. Instead, we need to eliminate the toxins that are poisoning their brains, whenever it is possible—and we need to do it quickly. Environmental medicine specialist Doris Rapp, M.D., stresses, "Children, in particular, have a limited, well-defined window of time during which they must acquire their education. If they are too ill or if their learning and/or behavior problems are too challenging, their education, career, or their future life may be seriously jeopardized."[32] And William Walsh, director of the Pfeiffer Center which successfully treats many "toxic" children (see Chapter 8), says it's critical to help children with metal imbalances before the teen years, when drugs, alcohol, school failure, and delinquent peers can set them unalterably on the wrong path.

"We have no trouble identifying future criminals," he says. "Our frustration is that nobody is listening to us."[33]

Notes

1 Moir, A. and Jessel, D. (1997) *A Mind to Crime*. London: Signet, p.198.
2 Details about this case are taken from an appeal filed by Hodges' attorneys.
3 Wilson, J. (1998) "The chemistry of violence." *Popular Mechanics 3*, 42–3.

4   Guillette, E.A., Meza, M.M., Aquilar, M.G., Soto, A.D. and Garcia, I.E. (1998) "An anthropological approach to the evaluation of preschool children exposed to pesticides in Mexico." *Environmental Health Perspectives 106*, 6, 347–53.

5   Study by Byers and Lord, cited by *Rachel's Environment and Health Weekly 529*, January 16, 1997.

6   Cited by Waldman, S. in "Lead and your kids." *Newsweek*, July 15, 1991.

7   Porter, W.P., Jaeger, J.W. and Carlson, I.H. (1999) "Endocrine, immune, and behavioral effects of aldicarb (carbamate), atrazine (triazine) and nitrate (fertilizer) mixtures at groundwater concentrations." *Toxicology and Industrial Health 15*, 1–2, 133–50.

8   (2006) "Epigenetics: Can your actions today affect your grandchildren's genes and behavior?" *Crime Times 12*, 2, 1–4.

9   "Study finds industrial pollution begins in the womb: Hundreds of toxic chemicals measured in newborn babies," news release, Environmental Working Group, July 14, 2005.

10 Jacobson, J. and Jacobson, S.W. (1996) "Intellectual impairment in children exposed to polychlorinated biphenyls in utero." *New England Journal of Medicine 335*, 11, 783–9; and Raloff, J. (1996) "Banned pollutant's legacy: Lower IQs." *Science News 150*, 11, September 14.

11 Raloff, J. (1996) "Banned pollutant's legacy: Lower IQs." *Science News 150*, 11, September 14.

12 Walkowiak, J., Wiener, J.A., Fastabend, A., Heinzow, B., Krämer, U., Schmidt, E., Steingrüber, H.-J., Wundram, S. and Winneke, G. (2001) "Environmental exposure to polychlorinated biphenyls and quality of the home environment: Effects on psychodevelopment in early childhood." *The Lancet 358*, 9293, 1602–7.

13 Landrigan, P., Claudio, L., Markowitz, S.B., Berkowitz, G.S., Brenner, B.L., Romero, H., Wetmur, J.G., Matte, T.D., Gore, A.C., Godbold, J.H. and Wolff, M.S. (1999) "Pesticides and inner-city children: Exposures, risks, and prevention." *Environmental Health Perspectives 107* (Suppl 3), 431–7.

14 Schumann S. (2002–03) "Monitoring the effects of pesticide exposure." *Occupational Health Tracker 5*, 4, 1.

15 Sood, B., Delaney-Black, V., Covington, C., Nordstrom-Klee, B., Ager, J., Templin, T., Janisse, J., Martier, S. and Sokol, R.J. (2001) "Prenatal alcohol exposure and childhood behavior at age 6 to 7 years: I. Dose-response effect." *Pediatrics 108*, 2, August, E34; and Mulvihill, K. (2001) "Even small amounts of alcohol in pregnancy harmful." *Reuters Health*, August 7.

16 Statistics cited in "Key facts on Fetal Alcohol Spectrum Disorder," FASWorld. Available at www.fasworld.com (accessed 10 October 2007).

17 Fergusson, D., Woodward, L. and Horwood, L.J. (1998) "Maternal smoking during pregnancy and psychiatric adjustment in late adolescence." *Archives of General Psychiatry 55*, 721–7.

18 Brennan, P.A., Grekin, E.R., Mortensen, E.L. and Mednick, S.A. (2002) "Relationship of maternal smoking during pregnancy with criminal arrest and hospitalization for substance abuse in male and female adult offspring." *American Journal of Psychiatry 159*, 1, 48–54.

19 Bellini, J. (1989) *High Tech Holocaust*. San Francisco: Sierra Club Books.

20 Weiss, B. (1983) "Behavioral toxicology and environmental health science." *American Psychologist 38*, 11, 1174–87.

21 Canfield, R.L., Henderson, Jr., C.R., Cory-Slechta, D.A., Cox, C., Jusko, T.A., and Lanphear, B. (2003) "Intellectual Impairment in Children with blood lead concentrations below 10 µg per deciliter." *New England Journal of Medicine 348*, 16, 1517–26.

22 Needleman, H.L., Schell, A., Bellinger, D., Leviton, A. and Allred, E. (1990) "The long-term effects of exposure to low doses of lead in childhood: An 11-year follow-up report." *New England Journal of Medicine 322*, 2, 83–8.

23 Needleman, H.L., McFarland, C., Ness, R.B., Fienberg, S.E. and Tobin, M.J. (2002) "Bone lead levels in adjudicated delinquents: A case control study." *Neurotoxicology and Teratology 24*, 6, 711–7.

24 Needleman, H.L., Riess, J., Tobin, M., Biesecker, G. and Greenhouse, J. (1996) "Bone lead levels and delinquent behavior." *Journal of the American Medical Association 275*, 5, 363–9.

25 Masters, R.D., Coplan, M.J., Hone, B.T. and Dykes, J.E. (2000) "Association of silicofluoride treated water with elevated blood lead." *Neurotoxicology 21*, 6, 1091–100.

26 Gugliotta, G. (2004) "Mercury threat to fetus raised: EPA revises risk estimates." *Washington Post*, February 6.

27 Pihl, R.O. and Parkes, M. (1977) "Hair element content of learning disabled children." *Science 198*, 204–6.

28 Pihl, R.O. and Ervin, F. (1990) "Lead and cadmium levels in violent criminals." *Psychological Reports 66*, 3, Pt. 1, 839–44.

29 "Environment may increase drug abuse." Press release, Texas A&M University, August 23, 2000.

30 Gottschalk, L.A., Rebello, T., Buchsbaum, M.S., Tucker, H.G. and Hodges, E.L. (1991) "Abnormalities in hair trace elements as indicators of aberrant behavior." *Comprehensive Psychiatry 32*, 3, 229–37.

31 Werbach, M.R. (1995) "Nutritional influences on aggressive behavior." *Journal of Orthomolecular Medicine 7*, 1, 45–51.

32 Rapp, D. (1996) *Is This Your Child's World?* New York: Bantam Books, p.30.

33 Personal communication.

CHAPTER 7

Medically Caused Dyslogic: When Drugs and Other Medical Treatments Damage the Brain

"First, do no harm."

—Hippocrates

"First, pharmaceutical companies thrive on illness, not on wellness. Their profits are staggering, and they have no financial incentive to strive for societal well-being… Second, most physicians have little training in nutrition and disease prevention; they are trained not to foster health, but to treat symptoms. The end result of these two factors is an illness-oriented medical industry, in which ineffective and even harmful treatments often flourish."

—Max Ricketts, *The Great Anxiety Escape*[1]

It's natural, when your child is sick, to turn to doctors for help. It's also natural to seek medical help in protecting your child from suffering from disease or injury. We have faith that doctors' training translates into a true understanding of the human body, and that our children's physicians always have their patients' best interests at heart.

That faith, unfortunately, is often misplaced.

Like most parents, I initially trusted in the wisdom and expertise of modern medicine. Decades of research, however, taught me that physicians all too often fail to cure illnesses, very frequently prescribe remedies that make patients far worse (or kill them), and—perhaps the most egregious offense—often create illness in perfectly well individuals.

The term for such illness is "iatrogenic," meaning induced by a medical professional's treatment, and it is far more common than most people think. Every year, for instance, more than 100,000 people are killed by prescription drugs (many prescribed to treat minor problems).[2] Moreover, a recent study found that up to 20 percent of all drugs approved by the FDA will, within 25 years, wind up being withdrawn from the market or given "black box" warnings indicating that they cause significant injury or death in many cases.[3] In excess of a million hospital patients, many of them hospitalized for minor and non-life-threatening conditions, die each year as a result of iatrogenic injury or illness. This is not surprising, when you learn that research consistently shows that only around 15 percent of medical treatments are "evidence based"—that is, can be supported as effective given current research—while virtually all carry serious risks.[4]

Nowhere are these risks more evident than among the most vulnerable of our population, our children. I've already discussed the dangers of psychiatric drugs, which usually address the symptoms rather than the causes of dyslogic, and often lead to aberrant, suicidal, or homicidal behavior (see Chapter 4). I've also discussed the widespread promotion by doctors of infant formulas that lack essential ingredients and can be toxic (see Chapter 5). But these may be merely the tip of the iceberg when it comes to damage inflicted on children by the medical profession sworn to protect them.

Indeed, there is growing evidence that many cases of childhood attention deficit hyperactivity disorder (ADHD), learning disabilities, antisocial behavior, and severe psychoses, such as autism and depression, stem directly from medical interventions—including one intervention that is not only sanctioned by the medical profession, but actually mandated.

In 1980, Barbara Loe Fisher's son, Chris, was a cheerful, contented, exceptionally bright two-year-old who could speak in full sentences and count up to 20. That all changed when his mother took him to the pediatrician for a diphtheria–pertussis–tetanus (DPT) shot and oral polio vaccination. A few hours after the shot, she walked into his room and found him sitting in a rocking chair, staring straight ahead "as if he couldn't see me standing in the doorway." His face was white and his lips were blue, and when Barbara called out to him, his eyes rolled back in his head and his head fell to his shoulder. "When I picked him up," she told a Congressional committee, "he was like a dead weight." He lay on his bed for six hours, and when Barbara woke him, he couldn't walk or speak coherently.

Over the following days, Chris deteriorated rapidly. He could no longer say the alphabet or count, wouldn't look at his picture books, and was listless and cried constantly. He had constant diarrhea, stopped growing, and developed chronic ear and respiratory infections. He seemed "spaced out," and sometimes drooled. Chris's pediatrician, however, said that it was "just a stage" and not to worry about it. Barbara took Chris to another pediatrician, who suggested cystic fibrosis or celiac disease, but tests came back negative. She says, "None of the doctors knew what was wrong with my son, who had become an entirely different child physically, mentally and emotionally."

A year later, Barbara discovered several articles in major medical journals describing reactions to pertussis vaccines. They matched her son's symptoms exactly. She learned that a British study had found a significant correlation between the DPT shot and brain inflammation leading to permanent neurological damage. She learned, too, that a study by UCLA and the Food and Drug Administration reported that 1 in 875 DPT shots is followed within two days by a convulsion or collapse/shock reaction similar to her son's.

"I was stunned," she told the hearing. "I felt betrayed by a medical profession I had revered all my life." Barbara asked why she hadn't been warned about the risks of the DPT shot, and about the possibility of a severe reaction—information that would have led her to recognize the symptoms of neurological dysfunction, and to

seek medical help. And later, as she continued to research the issue of vaccine damage, meeting hundreds of other vaccine-damaged children and their families in the process, she began to ask a larger question: "Has the increased administration of multiple vaccines in the first three years of life, when the brain and immune systems develop most rapidly, been an unrecognized co-factor in the epidemics of chronic disease and disability plaguing so many children today?"

Today, Barbara Loe Fisher is a leading expert on vaccine injury, and president and co-founder of the National Vaccine Information Center. Speaking of Chris, she says, "There is always the haunting vision of what could have been, intertwined with the certain knowledge that there is much to be thankful for. Both Chris and I know he was lucky compared to the children who have suffered vaccine reactions and been left quadriplegic, profoundly mentally retarded, epileptic, or have died." But "lucky" is a relative term. Now a young adult, Chris—labeled as gifted by one doctor when he was two—struggles to cope with cognitive problems that made it nearly impossible for him to finish high school. The legacy of his DPT shot includes minimal brain damage, fine motor and short-term memory delays, visual and auditory processing deficits, and attention deficit disorder.[5]

Barbara Loe Fisher's son Chris was perfectly normal before he received a DPT shot that changed his brain for life. She knows now, as she did not in 1980, that her son is only one of thousands of children drastically damaged by vaccines—and she suspects these children are only the tip of a very large iceberg, with many more children suffering from more subtle but still debilitating brain and nervous system damage. She is not alone in her suspicions.

A growing number of researchers around the world are questioning the safety of giving multiple immunizations to infants and very young children. The first vaccine discovered to be dangerous was the pertussis (whooping cough) component of the DPT or DTaP (acellular pertussis) vaccine, which can cause fevers as high as 106 degrees, seizures, brain damage, and sudden infant death syndrome. In one study of the DPT vaccine, says medical research journalist Neil Miller, "serious reactions (including grand mal epilepsy and encephalopathy) were shown to be as high as one in 600."[6] The newer DTaP shot containing acellular pertussis appears to be safer, but can cause all of the side effects of the DPT shot, up to and including death. (The death rate among babies is eight times greater than normal during the three-day period after receiving a pertussis shot.)[7]

These short-term effects are frightening enough, but what alarms researchers even more is the possibility that hundreds of thousands of children who exhibit only mild symptoms at the time of a DPT or DTaP shot may suffer severe long-term consequences. Medical historian Harris Coulter, Ph.D., who has studied vaccines for many years, implicates the DPT shot as a cause of wide-spread "post-encephalitic syndrome" in children. (Indeed, he notes, the pertussis vaccine is used to *induce* encephalitis (brain inflamation) in lab animals for research purposes!) Coulter's research indicates that the DPT shot causes a minimum of 12,000 cases of severe neurological damage every year, and he notes, "If there are 12,000 cases of severe neurological damage every year, there must be hundreds of thousands of cases of milder damage." This hidden damage, Coulter says, can take the form of learning disabilities, criminality, aberrant sexual behavior, attacks of rage, and mental illness.[8]

Scientists have long known that encephalitis, including subclinical encephalitis that causes no *apparent* long-term physical effects, can radically alter personality and behavior. Investigative medical writer Greg Wilson quotes a doctor describing the effects of brain inflammation on one child who survived a massive wave of a strep-linked disorder called *encephalitis lethargica* in the early 1900s:

> The moral aspect of his behavior has been emphasized, naturally enough, as it is his apparent disregard of all moral considerations that makes him impossible at home, at school, or in the sick ward; and many have professed to see in this an absence, a numbing, or a perversion of his moral sense.[9]

Researchers Sarah Cheyette and Jeffrey Cummings, investigating the same epidemic, note that thousands of children who contracted *encephalitis lethargica*—children who had, in general, exhibited no psychiatric problems before their illness—became, literally, different people:

> They became disobedient and quarrelsome, often leading to expulsion from school. Emotional lability, irritability, and temper tantrums were common. Many children committed destructive and harmful acts on people or animals; self-destructive behavior was also common. Kleptomania, pyromania, coprolalia [swearing], sexual precocity, exhibitionism, sexual aggression, and paraphilias [fetishism, sadism, voyeurism, etc.] were manifestations of the behavioral disorder. Many children felt compelled to perform these acts even though they recognized them as "bad" behavior. The children were hyperactive and impulsive, and they appeared to lack empathy; they were often called "moral imbeciles."[10]

I believe it is no coincidence that these descriptions sound remarkably similar to the behaviors exhibited by millions of dyslogical children today. Given that vaccines are known to have caused attacks of encephalitis in thousands of children, and that they cause symptoms resembling subclinical encephalitis (drowsiness, irritability, abnormal sleep patterns, bizarre crying or screaming spells) in millions more, we might expect to see the personality changes that appeared in children with *encephalitis lethargica* occurring today in large numbers of children who've received DPT shots—and we do. The *encephalitis lethargica* epidemic of the early 1900s created thousands of feral, amoral, and disturbed children. It is distinctly possible that we, through our well-intentioned vaccination programs, are creating many thousands more.

But the DPT is not the only vaccine linked to serious brain dysfunction or damage. At the same time that Barbara Loe Fisher began investigating the link between the DPT and learning and behavior problems, I began noticing a separate trend—this one involving autism. When I'd first started studying autism, back in the late 1950s and early 1960s, the disorder was rare. Then, beginning in the 1970s, a strange thing happened: the numbers of autistic children began growing, at first slowly and then, as the decades went by, more and more swiftly. By the late 1980s or early 1990s, I began to suspect that the increase wasn't merely due to better diagnosis—that, for some unknown reason, the rates of autism were skyrocketing.

A decade later, the increase was too obvious to ignore. Figures from California in 2002 revealed a 12,300 percent *increase* in the rate of autism since the state began keeping records in 1971, and nationally the rate of autism had soared from 5 in 10,000 children in 1970 to 20 in 10,000 (and, according to some research, is now as high as 1 in 166 children). England, Canada, Israel, and other developed countries reported similar explosions in their autism rates.

Moreover, the vast majority of newer cases involved children who appeared normal at birth and then regressed at around 18 months. This rise in late-onset autism, in the absence of a correspondingly steep rise in early-onset autism (which increased at a far slower pace), clearly pointed to environmental influences. While autism also involves genetic vulnerability, genes can't suddenly cause a catastrophic increase in a particular disease—unless an environmental trigger is involved.

And autism, as I've noted, wasn't the only disorder that became epidemic at the end of the twentieth century. At the same time, we witnessed an alarming rise in the number of cases of attention deficit hyperactivity disorder (ADHD), childhood depression, conduct disorder, learning disabilities, and related disorders. In addition, as noted in Chapter 2, we saw a continuing decline in the performance of "normal" children over the past few decades, when compared to the performance of children born in earlier decades.

I knew that nutritional, environmental, and medical pollution were to blame, to a large extent, for this rise in "dyslogic disorders." I was also aware of Harris Coulter's research strongly implicating the DPT shot as a cause of brain damage and aberrant behavior. But when I and other researchers began studying the autism epidemic in particular, another interesting pattern came to light.

Starting in about 1930, and continuing through 2002, many of the vaccines given to infants and toddlers contained a preservative, thimerosal, which is nearly 50 percent mercury—one of the most toxic substances on earth. Over the years, as the number of shots given to infants rose from three to more than 30, the amount of mercury being injected into these children's bodies rose enormously. Eventually, although none of the officials mandating these vaccines took the trouble to notice, the quantities of mercury given to children via vaccinations exceeded the Environmental Protection Agency's allowable level for total average mercury exposure from all sources. And as children's exposure to thimerosal rose, the rates of autism rose almost in lockstep.

In retrospect, it's remarkable that it took researchers so long to identify the link between thimerosal and autism. Mercury causes abnormal migration of neurons in the developing brain, alters brain chemicals, and impairs immune system function (contributing to autoimmune attacks on the nervous system and to an impaired ability to fight diseases that can damage the brain). Mercury also damages the intestines, weakening the body's defenses against viruses, bacteria, and pathogenic yeasts, and allowing neuroactive peptides (including certain opium-like substances) to escape into the bloodstream. Is it any surprise that injecting large amounts of this toxic heavy metal directly into children's bodies could damage their brains sufficiently to make them autistic?

One large government-funded study of thimerosal—initially "buried" by the Centers for Disease Control and Prevention, which released it only under pressure—looked into the effects of thimerosal exposure during infancy. The version of the study released to the public stated that there was no risk associated with mercury exposure, but the confidential version found a 2.48 times increased risk of autism. In the U.S., courts of law generally accept that a relative increased risk of 2.0 or higher is sufficient to substantiate that a given exposure causes disease.[11] Another study found that, when compared to children given mercury-free DTaP shots, children given mercury-containing DTaP shots had a six-fold increase in the risk of autism, a six-fold increase in the risk of mental retardation, and a two-fold increase in the risk of having speech disorders.[12]

More recent laboratory studies show clear evidence that even small amounts of thimerosal can harm the brain. Richard Deth and colleagues, for example, found that thimerosal interferes with methylation (a process critical to normal neurological development). Deth and his coworkers speculate that thimerosal-induced methylation deficits play a role in both autism and ADHD.[13] A separate study, this one by researchers at UC Davis, found that exposure to even tiny amounts of thimerosal can dramatically alter the function of dendritic cells, which play a key role in immune system function.[14] There is evidence that a particular subset of children, who lack the ability to clear toxic metals from their bodies efficiently due to their genetic makeup, are at highest risk for mercury damage.[15]

You will not hear about these findings from official government agencies, which typically reassure parents that vaccines are perfectly safe. These agencies play up epidemiological studies, which are a very blunt instrument that cannot detect damage when it occurs only in a vulnerable subgroup of the population. More importantly, the research on which government agencies' conclusions about vaccine safety are based is contaminated to the point of uselessness by the fact that many of the researchers are on the payrolls of vaccine companies—and the fact that the Centers for Disease Control, the Food and Drug Administration, and the National Institutes of Health all have a strong vested interest in supporting the status quo when it comes to vaccines.

Does that sound paranoid? Here are the words of U.S. Congressman Dave Weldon, an M.D., who has been investigating the vaccine controversy:

> I am very concerned about the number of reports I continue to receive from researchers regarding their difficulties in pursuing answers to questions about the possible association between vaccines or vaccine components and the epidemic of autism. Some report overt discouragement, intimidation and threats, and have abandoned this field of research. Some have had their clinical privileges revoked and others have been hounded out of their institutions.[16]

Congressman Dan Burton, a member of the House Committee on Government Reform, is equally angered by government agencies' foot-dragging when it comes to making vaccine data available to independent researchers—including stall tactics such as providing researchers with blank databases. Rather than trying to investigate the potential dangers of vaccines, Burton charges, it appears that government agencies intend to "do the bare minimum that they have to do to get us off their backs."[17]

That obstruction has almost undoubtedly translated into thousands more ruined lives. Says Stephanie Cave, M.D.:

> The injection of mercury appears to affect only certain children, but I fear that we have underestimated the devastation by concentrating on the autistic children. We are measuring elevated levels of mercury in other children with milder difficulties like learning disabilities, ADHD, and Asperger's Syndrome [a milder variant of autism]. We do not have any idea what the scope of this problem is at this point.[18]

Mercury-free shots are now available, and have been for several years (although many doctors continued to use stockpiles of mercury-containing vaccines well after the mercury-free vaccines became available). The early results of the switch to mercury-free shots are striking: in California, a state which keeps very accurate statistics on autism rates, *the steep increase in new cases of autism has suddenly and dramatically reversed.* In fact, autism rates in California dropped every year between 2003 and 2005, after rising for a decade.

David Kirby, a *New York Times* investigative reporter whose book *Evidence of Harm* uncovered the government's attempts to downplay the dangers of thimerosal, commented at the beginning of 2005, "This very decline, at this very moment, has long been predicted by supporters of the thimerosal-autism theory." He added, "If the numbers in California and elsewhere continue to drop—and that is still a big if—the implication of thimerosal in the autism epidemic will be practically undeniable."[19]

However, the damage caused to an entire generation of children exposed to dangerous levels of this heavy metal is incalculable. Moreover, vaccines still contain other toxins, including aluminum and formaldehyde, and the viral agents used in vaccines can themselves cause damage. Among recent alarming findings about the effects of vaccines:

- Andrew Wakefield, M.D., and his colleagues report finding a strong link between the measles–mumps–rubella (MMR) vaccine and a syndrome involving regressive autism and a unique form of inflammatory bowel disease (IBD). Many of the autistic children with this never-before-seen form of IBD show evidence of chronic measles infection stemming from vaccination.[20] (While it is beyond the scope of this book, the "trashing" of Dr. Wakefield's reputation is an excellent illustration of the power of the forces attempting to quell research into the risks of vaccines. I refer interested readers to a February 23, 2004 story in Britain's *Daily Mail*, aptly entitled "The smearing of Andrew Wakefield," which details the ordeal that this remarkable physician has undergone.) Other researchers are now reporting this once-unknown form of bowel disorder in children with ADHD, indicating that the measles vaccine plays a role in ADHD as well as autism.[21]

- The federal government's Vaccine Adverse Event Reporting System (VAERS), which supposedly documents adverse reactions to vaccines, received nearly 10,000 reports involving the chickenpox vaccine between March 1995 and December 1999. These reactions included brain inflammation, neurological damage, immune system abnormalities, seizures, and death.[22] It's important to note, by the way, that since reporting adverse events is not mandatory, only an estimated 1 to 10 percent of adverse events are reported to the VAERS.

Clearly, the evidence cries out for research on the potential dangers of vaccines—far more research than the handful of studies, most of them funded by vaccine manufacturers with gross financial conflicts of interest, that have been conducted by the U.S. government. Among the issues that must be addressed:

- *What are the long-term effects of vaccination?* In addition to elevating the risk of neurological disorders, vaccinations are tentatively linked to increasing rates of diabetes, arthritis, Crohn's disease, and autoimmune disorders.

- *What are the risk/benefit ratios for vaccines?* Increasingly, doctors are immunizing children against relatively minor illnesses, such as chickenpox—a questionable decision, in light of the evidence linking vaccination to rising rates of serious mental and physical disorders. Moreover, children are being vaccinated for diseases such as hepatitis B, which only a tiny percentage of children are likely to contract. And rates of many diseases for which children are immunized were actually dropping *before* widespread immunization began.

- *What are the effects of the toxic substances in vaccines?* What happens when we inject children with formaldehyde, aluminum, live viruses, or contaminants such as avian reverse transcriptase? What happens, moreover, when we inject children with a "cocktail" of multiple vaccines on a single day?

- *Are vaccines particularly dangerous for children at high risk for neurological disorder*—for instance, "preemies," children with previous bad reactions to vaccines, or children with a family history of neurological or immune disease? Also, are vaccines particularly dangerous when given to very young infants whose bodies are not yet able to efficiently eliminate the toxins in vaccines?

- *Do vaccines, which stimulate some elements of the immune system excessively while bypassing other elements, "skew" immune function* in ways that contribute both to autoimmune disease and to a reduced ability to fight natural infections?

With vaccines now mandated for virtually every American child, these are questions that need answers—but those answers aren't likely to come from the government. Indeed, the government and vaccine manufacturers appear to be on a quest to vaccinate every child against every known disease, no matter what the consequences. Barbara Loe Fisher, whose son's story began this chapter, notes with dismay, "There are more than 200 experimental vaccines being developed to prevent everything from tooth decay to stomach ulcers, as well as a super-vaccine to be given at birth that will inject raw DNA from 20 to 30 different viruses and bacteria directly into the cells of newborns."[23]

Will these vaccines create the disease-free utopia that mass-vaccination advocates promise—or will they add to our burgeoning epidemic of dyslogic, autism, learning disabilities, delinquency, depression, and hyperactivity? Given our ever-rising rates of mental illness, childhood diabetes, asthma, and other disorders since mass immunization programs began, I see little reason to be optimistic.

Dyslogic in the delivery room

The link between vaccines and dyslogic is alarming, but the damage done to babies' brains by the medical profession often begins well before the first vaccination. In fact, the delivery room itself is one of the most dangerous places a baby will ever see. That's because doctors have taken a routine, natural event—childbirth—and transformed it into a high-tech, drug-intensive, unnatural procedure, in which the doctor's comfort and convenience often supersede the safety of either mother or infant.

Does that sound harsh? If so, consider the example of Cytotec (misoprostol), a drug used to induce labor.

Cytotec is a relatively new drug that was approved by the FDA for treating ulcers, not for the induction of labor. However, doctors soon discovered that the drug's side effects include violent uterine cramping, severe enough to cause miscarriages. You might think this would lead physicians to question the safety of the drug as an ulcer treatment. Instead, it led them to begin using Cytotec to induce or accelerate labor contractions.

There are times, of course, when inducing labor is necessary—for instance, if a fetus is dangerously large or extremely overdue. But when a woman's pregnancy and labor are perfectly normal, as is the case for most women given Cytotec, it's a very bad idea. For one thing, despite modern technology, we can't really tell how fully developed an unborn baby is, so when labor is induced, there's a risk that the baby will be delivered too early. For another, natural labor sets off a cascade of chemical changes that help facilitate everything from maternal milk production to infant–mother bonding. Rushing this process unnecessarily can have long-term consequences, none of them good.

However, these dangers pale when compared to the potential dangers of Cytotec itself. Only a handful of studies have been conducted on the use of Cytotec to induce labor, but those studies show that the drug can cause fetal tachycardia (rapid heart rate) and other signs of distress, and can cause the uterus to rupture, causing severe and possibly fatal damage to both mother and baby. Because of these risks, the Cochrane Collaboration, an international group of physicians and researchers that analyzes the effectiveness of various drug treatments, concluded that Cytotec "cannot be recommended for routine use at this stage."[24]

Yet according to the American College of Obstetricians and Gynecologists, one in five labors are now induced, and Cytotec is the preferred labor-inducing drug. Why? It's cheap, at as little as 13 cents a dose. Also, unlike Pitocin, the former labor-inducing drug of choice, Cytotec can be used even with women whose cervixes aren't "ripe," making it particularly convenient. Marsden Wagner, M.D., a critic of the rampant use of Cytotec, comments that an Oregon doctor:

> told me (and repeated it on her local weekly *TV Health* program) that obstetricians in Medford told her they are thrilled with Cytotec for induction because they can bring women in first thing in the morning, give them Cytotec and have the babies out before 5 p.m.—a welcome return to daylight obstetrics.[25]

In short, doctors are giving women a drug that can endanger both mother and baby, usually in the absence of any good reason, simply because it allows them to deliver babies when the doctors find it convenient to do it. As a result, the numbers of babies born during Monday-through-Friday daylight hours are disproportionately higher than the numbers born at night or on weekends. This is wonderful news for doctors whose chief concern is getting a good night's sleep. It also helps a doctor's bottom line. Says midwife and Cytotec critic Ina May Gaskin, "Cytotec's great claim to fame—prompt, timely labors—is phenomenal boon [since] in most cases an obstetrician must be present at the time the baby is born to be paid in full for a birth."[26] But it's not wonderful news for the babies whose brains are damaged by an unnecessary procedure and an unnecessary drug.

Melissa Emerine told a Silicon Valley Metro reporter that, shortly after receiving a dose of Cytotec, "I began having severe chest pains and my arms went numb. It felt like an elephant sitting on my chest." When doctors performed an emergency Caesarean section, they found that Emerine's uterus had torn as a result of her forceful induced contractions, and the baby was outside of the womb. The infant, Delaney, was deprived of oxygen for ten minutes and now has cerebral palsy.[27]

Again, the children with severe damage due to Cytotec may be only a small portion of those injured by the drug, because for every infant who suffers cerebral palsy or dies due to the drug, it's likely that many more are subtly harmed. Given the dearth of research on long-term effects of Cytotec on exposed infants, we may never know.

A number of doctors who do not use Cytotec regularly use Pitocin, a labor-inducing drug that's been used for years. But Pitocin does not have a clean bill of health, either. Eric Hollander, M.D., of Mt. Sinai Medical Center, reported several years ago that 60 percent of the autistic patients in his clinic had been exposed to Pitocin before birth, compared to 20 percent of children in the general population.[28] His findings parallel those of an earlier Japanese study that found a much higher incidence of autism among children whose mothers received Pitocin and anesthesia during delivery than among children of mothers not exposed to these drugs.[29]

Labor-inducing drugs, however, are only one potentially dangerous intervention that's often used before or during labor and delivery. Other drugs and technologies that can put the fetus at risk for later dyslogic include the following.

Terbutaline. This drug, an asthma medication that can temporarily stop preterm contractions, is not approved by the Food and Drug Administration for use as a treatment for preterm labor, and the drug has never been formally tested for this purpose. In 1997, the FDA issued a letter cautioning doctors against prescribing terbutaline to pregnant women for extended periods, noting that the drug had been shown to be effective only at delaying premature labor for 48 hours or less, and warning that its effects on fetal development were largely

unknown. However, the drug—frequently administered by subcuta-
neous pump—is currently being used as a long-term treatment for up
to a quarter of a million pregnant women annually. Yet growing
research reveals that it is a potent developmental neurotoxin.

Melissa Rhodes and colleagues recently administered terbutaline
to neonatal rats at a developmental stage similar to that of late fetal
development in humans. The researchers report that the drug caused
biochemical changes indicative of injury to brain cells, and that further
evaluation revealed structural abnormalities in three brain regions (the
cerebellum, hippocampus, and somatosensory cortex). "These effects,"
Rhodes and colleagues say, "point to a causal relationship between
fetal terbutaline exposure and the higher incidence of cognitive and
neuropsychiatric disorders reported for the offspring of women
receiving terbutaline therapy for preterm labor."[30]

In related research, Rhodes *et al.* found that rats exposed to
terbutaline during the neonatal period experienced brain changes that
made them abnormally susceptible later in life to the harmful effects of
the organophosphate insecticide chlorpyrifos (CFS). "You could see
the biochemical evidence of the damage early on," says Theodore
Slotkin, a member of the research team. "The functional and structural
changes emerged or were evidenced in adolescence or adulthood."

This finding, the research team concludes, suggests that
"terbutaline, like chlorpyrifos, is a developmental neurotoxicant, and
that its use in the therapy of preterm labor may create a subpopulation
that is sensitized to the adverse neural effects of a subsequent exposure
to organophosphate insecticides."[31]

Demerol, a narcotic given as a painkiller during labor. Midwife
Beverley Lawrence Beech notes that Demerol readily crosses the
placenta and can depress the fetal respiratory system if a dose is given
two or three hours before birth. Because the baby's liver is immature,
Beech points out, it takes a long time—18 to 23 hours—for the drug
to be cleared from the system. She notes that mothers who breastfeed
often give their babies a second dose of Demerol through their breast
milk.[32]

Amazingly, there is almost no research on the effects of exposing
infants to large amounts of a narcotic such as Demerol. However, one

large-scale study, done decades ago, came to alarming conclusions. Yvonne Brackbill and Sarah Broman, evaluating the children of 3500 healthy mothers with uncomplicated pregnancies,[33] found that children of the mothers who took pain-killing drugs tended to lag in their ability to sit, stand, or move about, and that their behavior was affected at least through age seven. Brackbill and Broman say exposed children were slow in developing mental skills such as talking and reading, and had trouble stopping a behavior such as crying once they started. This inability to cease a behavior once it is started, known as perseveration, is seen in many children with brain dysfunction.

Epidural (local) anesthesia. Epidurals, used in the majority of deliveries, slow the labor process and thus put infants at greater risk for infection and fetal distress. Also, because epidurals can make it difficult for a mother to push efficiently, they increase the risk of cesarean section delivery by 10 percent. In addition, epidural anesthesia can cause bradycardia (decreased heart rate) in the fetus,[34] and can increase the need for the use of instruments such as forceps that can cause brain injury.

Prenatal ultrasound. Prenatal ultrasound exams can save lives and allow for early detection of medical problems, and they have an important place in medical care. However, some experts are raising concerns over the widespread use of these tests, often for no good medical reason. (For example, you can now get a prenatal ultrasound, along with a souvenir "portrait" of your unborn child, at some shopping malls). Dr. Wagner notes,

> Some research has shown the possibility that ultrasound can cause slowed growth of the fetus while still in the uterus. Other research has shown the possibility that some children who have been scanned while still in the uterus may later have mild neurological deficits.[35]

A 2006 study of pregnant mice raised additional red flags, when it reported that prolonged ultrasound scans interfered with the migration of some neurons to their proper positions in the developing mouse embryo. Study co-author Pasko Rakic commented, "When cells are in the wrong place, they might affect function of the cerebral cortex... We just don't know yet what this could do."[36]

Unnecessary cesarean section deliveries. The Public Citizen Health Research Group estimates that half of the nearly one million cesarean sections performed every year are medically unnecessary. Babies delivered by cesarean section are more likely to develop respiratory distress syndrome (because the normal birth process removes more fluid from the baby's lungs than does a C-section delivery), and more likely to be delivered prematurely—a strong risk factor for learning disabilities and behavior disorders.

Who benefits from high-tech delivery?

Marsden Wagner notes that 50 to 80 percent of births in typical U.S. hospitals involve one or more surgical procedures, "further proof that obstetricians have turned birth into a surgical event." Far from being beneficial to babies, this over-medicalization of a normal physiological process is highly dangerous to their health. One study of low-risk births found that, compared to those births overseen by physicians, those overseen by midwives result in 33 percent fewer deaths among newborns, and 31 percent fewer low-birthweight babies.[37]

Indeed, the evidence reveals that obstetricians frequently administer drugs or use artificial interventions to benefit themselves, not mothers or their infants. In a recent study, researchers evaluated the records of more than 37,000 children born in Philadelphia hospitals over a three-year period. All of the mothers included in the study were in normal, non-induced labor when admitted, and the researchers excluded any cases in which fetal distress or lengthy or abnormal labor occurred.

The researchers compared the number of medical interventions used during the hospitals' "peak" hours (10 a.m. to 10 p.m.) to the number used during the "off-peak" hours of 2 a.m. to 8 a.m. They found that women who gave birth during the peak hours were 86 percent more likely to be given drugs, and 43 percent more likely to have a delivery involving the use of forceps or a vacuum extractor. In addition, they were more likely to have an episiotomy, and they were also more likely to experience vaginal tearing.

The researchers conclude that the differences in peak and off-peak treatment may stem from:

increased pressures on doctors and hospital staff to 'clear' patients at times when they have other patients to see... Busy doctors in busy hospitals may simply have less tolerance for the otherwise time-consuming natural progression of labor and delivery during these times.[38]

That lack of tolerance, unfortunately, translates into babies damaged by unnecessary medical procedures, and babies whose brains and bodies are stressed by the violent labor induced by drugs. The few hours that doctors save in the delivery room by using these technologies in situations where they are not medically warranted can translate into decades of suffering for children who experience brain damage or dysfunction as a result of dangerous and unneeded interventions, a trade-off to which few informed parents would agree.

One wonders what Hippocrates, who cautioned doctors to "first do no harm," would think of doctors who deliberately increase their patients' risk of injury or death—not in an effort to treat them, but simply in an effort to get to bed on time.

Infancy and beyond: the role of antibiotics and other drugs in dyslogic

In 1981, Duffy Mayo, the son of Gianna and Gus Mayo of San Francisco, was three and a half years old. Duffy initially was a bright and active youngster, learning to speaking both English and Italian before he mysteriously began to regress, losing his skills and developing severe symptoms of autism.

After two specialists made a diagnosis of autism, the Mayos were lucky enough to take Duffy to allergist Alan Levin in their search for help. Levin found that Duffy's immune system was severely impaired. What interested Levin most was the fact that Duffy had been given a number of treatments with antibiotics, which were intended to control his ear infections. Levin knew that such antibiotics often kill the microorganisms that compete with candida in the human body and thus allow candida to grow to overwhelming proportions.

Levin treated Duffy with Nystatin. Duffy at first got worse (a common reaction, caused by the toxins released by the dying candida cells). Then he began to improve. Since candida thrives on certain foods (especially sugars and refined carbohydrates) Duffy's diet required extensive modification. By the time he was ten, Duffy was an active, greatly improved child with few remaining signs of autism. His immune system was still impaired, however, and he still required treatment.

After birth, almost all children in Western countries are routinely exposed to another category of drugs that can cause dyslogic: antibiotics. These drugs, indeed, can save lives (although their overuse is making them increasingly less useful in combating infections). However, whether used appropriately or inappropriately, antibiotics can wreak havoc on the beneficial flora of the digestive tract—and since the brain and the gut are intimately interlinked (see Chapter 5), they can indirectly impair brain function and cause dyslogical behavior in children.

What happens when you give a child a course of antibiotics? If you're lucky, the drugs kill the bacteria they're intended to defeat—but they also kill off helpful lactobacillus and other needed microorganisms. When doctors give repeated doses of antibiotics (for instance, in the case of a resistant ear infection'), still more beneficial flora die, allowing the bowel to become overgrown with candida yeast and other potentially pathogenic fungi. In abnormally large numbers, these normally controlled organisms produce toxic and mind-altering byproducts. The result: symptoms ranging from a "drunken" appearance to hyperactivity or even autism.

The late William Crook, M.D., an expert on candida-linked psychiatric symptoms, said, "Children with ADHD often give a history of repeated ear infections in infancy. Such ear problems are usually treated with amoxicillin and/or other broad-spectrum antibiotic drugs. A research study found that 69 percent of children being evaluated for

---

*   Ear infections are caused by viruses and not bacteria in many cases, so the antibiotics
         are rarely effective.

school failure who were receiving medication for hyperactivity gave a history of greater than ten ear infections. By contrast, only 20 percent of non-hyperactive children had more than ten infections." He says this isn't surprising, given that "Candida puts out toxins which affect the nervous system, the immune system and other parts of the body."[39]

A questionnaire I sent out many years ago to parents asked what drugs made their autistic children's behavior either better or worse. Interestingly, Ritalin, the drug most often used then, scored near the bottom of the list in the "better" department, as did most of the psychiatric drugs commonly prescribed at the time. But what surprised me more was that Nystatin, a treatment for yeast infections, scored very, very high—while antibiotics made the children's behavior *much* worse. Since that time, I've spoken with hundreds of parents and professionals who report cases involving children whose behavior worsened after chronic exposure to antibiotics, and improved dramatically after treatment to combat the resulting yeast overgrowth.

Antibiotics, however, aren't the only drugs that can change children's biochemistry in ways that cause them to act "crazy" or dyslogical. In Chapter 4, I discussed how psychiatric drugs often make children's behavior far worse, rather than better. But a host of other drugs, most seemingly having nothing to do with the brain or behavior, can make kids act bizarrely, think poorly, or suffer from attention problems. In *Prescription for Disaster,* Thomas J. Moore notes that 399 drugs can cause asthenia (weakness), 242 can cause depression, 229 can cause malaise, 239 can cause anxiety, 325 can cause nervousness, and 314 can cause confusion.[40] These drugs include everything from antibiotics and antihistamines to blood pressure drugs and steroids.

Yet doctors often prescribe powerful drugs indiscriminately for children, rarely bothering to inform parents about the possible side effects. Some of these drugs are necessary, but many aren't. Worse yet, doctors prescribe drugs that have never been tested on children, simply guessing at the correct dosages. And they have little knowledge themselves about what any drug does; as the late Sydney Walker, M.D., said:

> Most physicians spend only three months in medical school learning about drugs and how they work. Once they're out of medical school,

doctors tend to rely on drug company representatives, hardly a source of unbiased information, to fill them in on new drugs. Even doctors who keep up religiously with medical journals don't get a clear picture of drug risks, because most research printed in medical journals focuses on the benefits of drugs, not their risks.[41]

Physicians, however, aren't the only culprits in the over-drugging of America's children. As consumers, we're conditioned to believe that visits to the doctor must conclude with the ritual writing of prescriptions, and if we don't come home with a bottle of pills, many of us feel that our doctors haven't done their jobs.

As a result, many of our children are over-drugged, taking cocktails of antibiotics, steroids, antihistamines, and other potentially behavior-altering medications, often topped off by psychoactive drugs such as Ritalin or antidepressants. As I noted in Chapter 4, these drugs are "toximolecular"—they are sub-lethal doses of toxic substances, alien to the body, given to suppress symptoms. But in the overwhelming majority of cases these symptoms stem from preventable, treatable, or even curable problems, ranging from the allergies and sensitivities I discussed in Chapter 5 (which are common causes of ear pain and "asthma" symptoms) to toxic exposure and dietary problems. It makes far more sense to detect these problems and treat them, than it does to mask their symptoms with drugs that can alter brain chemistry in dangerous ways.

While I've listed a litany of ways in which doctors damage young patients, sometimes beginning even before birth, it would be unjust to leave readers with the impression that all doctors cause harm to the children they treat. I've had the opportunity to work with hundreds of doctors who oppose drugging children, shooting them full of vaccines containing toxic heavy metals, and subjecting them to chemically induced, technologically controlled births. These doctors advocate safe and sane treatments—including healthful diets, the removal of toxins from the environment, and natural childbirth methods—in order to create healthy babies and children, to keep them healthy as they grow, and to cure their illnesses in ways that do not endanger their bodies or minds.

Unfortunately, these doctors are still in the minority, and their efforts to educate the medical community about working *with* patients' bodies, rather than fighting those bodies with toxic drugs and technologies, often fall on deaf ears. But their numbers are growing—and, more important, the numbers of consumers seeking them out is growing as well. It is up to these consumers to vote with their feet, and cast those votes in favor of safe, natural treatment—and against the unnatural medical practices that lead to "iatrogenic dyslogic."

Notes

1   Ricketts, M. (1990) *The Great Anxiety Escape.* La Mesa, CA: Matulungin Publishing, p.121.

2   Moore, T.J. (1998) *Prescription for Disaster.* New York: Dell.

3   Lasser, K.E., Allen, P.D., Woolhandler, S.J., Himmelstein, D.U., Wolfe, S.M. and Bor, D.H. (2002) "Timing of new black box warnings and withdrawals for prescription medications." *Journal of the American Medical Association 287,* 17, 2215–20.

4   Smith, R. (1992) "The ethics of ignorance." *Journal of Medical Ethics 18,* p.117.

5   Statement by Barbara Loe Fisher to the Institute of Medicine Immunization Safety Committee, January 11, 2001. Available at www.nvic.org/Loe_Fisher/blftestimony_iom_safety.htm (accessed 27 September 2007).

6   Miller, N.Z. (1993) *Vaccines: Are They Really Safe and Effective?* Santa Fe, NM: New Atlantean Press, p.47.

7   Ibid.

8   Coulter, H. (1990) *Vaccination, Social Violence, and Criminality: The Medical Assault on the American Brain.* Berkeley, CA: North Atlantic Books.

9   Wilson, G. (2000) *Vaccination and Behavioral Disorders.* Australia: Tuntable Creek Publishing, p.118.

10   Cheyette, S.R. and Cummings, J.L. (1995) "Encephalitis lethargica: Lessons for contemporary neuropsychiatry." *Journal of Neuropsychiatry and Clinical Neurosciences 7,* 2, 125–34.

11   This confidential CDC report, issued internally in 2001, was made public by the legal firm of Waters & Kraus.

12   Geier, M.R. and Geier, D.A. (2003) "Neurodevelopmental disorders after thimerosal-containing vaccines: A brief communication." *Journal of Experimental Biology and Medicine 228,* 6, 660–4.

13   Waly, M., Olteanu, H., Banerjee, R., Choi, S.W., Mason, J.B., Parker, B.S., Sukumar, S., Shim, S., Sharma, A., Benzecry, J.M., Power-Charnitsky, V.A. and Deth, R.C. (2004) "Activation of methionine synthase by insulin-like growth factor-1 and dopamine: A target for neurodevelopmental toxins and thimerosal." *Molecular Psychiatry 9,* 4, 358–70.

14   Goth, S.R., Chu, R.A., Gregg, J.P., Cherednichenko, G. and Pessah, I.N. (2006)
     "Uncoupling of ATP-mediated calcium signaling and dysregulated IL-6 secretion
     in dendritic cells by nanomolar thimerosal." *Environmental Health Perspectives 114*,
     7, 1083–91.

15   Bradstreet, J., Geier, D.A., Kartzinel, J.J., Adams, J.B. and Geier, M.R. (2003) "A
     case-control study of mercury burden in children with autistic spectrum
     disorders." *Journal of American Physicians and Surgeons 8*, 3, 76–9.

16   Keynote address to the Defeat Autism Now! (DAN!) Conference, Washington,
     D.C., April 16, 2004.

17   Burton's remarks were made at a June 19, 2002 hearing of the House Committee
     on Government Reform, chaired by Congressman Burton.

18   Cave, S. (2000) Testimony before the House Committee on Government Reform,
     July 18.

19   Kirby, D. (2005) "Autism, mercury and the California numbers." *Huffington Post*,
     July 13.

20   Ashwood, P., Murch, S.H., Anthony, A., Pellicer, A.A., Torrente, F., Thomson,
     M.A., Walker-Smith, J.A. and Wakefield, A.J. (2003) "Intestinal lymphocyte popu-
     lations in children with regressive autism: Evidence for extensive mucosal
     immunopathology." *Journal of Clinical Immunology 23*, 6, 504–17.

21   Sabra, S., Bellanti, J.A. and Colon, A.R. (1998) "Ileal lymphoid nodular hyperpla-
     sia, non-specific colitis, and pervasive developmental disorder in children." *The
     Lancet 352*, 234–5.

22   *The Chickenpox Vaccine: What You Should Know*, pamphlet produced by the
     ThinkTwice Global Vaccine Institute.

23   Testimony of Barbara Loe Fisher, Co-founder and President, National Vaccine
     Information Center, before the California Senate Committee on Health and
     Human Services hearing on "Childhood Immunization Mandates: Politics vs.
     Public Health," January 23, 2002.

24   Cited by Stein, L. in "Uninformed consent," MetroActive (online), March 21,
     2002.

25   Wagner, M. (1999) "Misoprostol (Cytotec) for labor induction: A cautionary tale."
     Midwifery Today 49, Spring.

26   Gaskin, I.M. (2000) "Cytotec: Dangerous experiment or panacea?" *Salon*, July 11.

27   Cited by Stein, L. in "Uninformed Consent," MetroActive (online), March 21,
     2002. Available at www.metroactive.com/papers/metro/0312.html (accessed 12
     October 2007).

28   Hollander's statistics were cited by Cowley, G. in "Understanding autism."
     Newsweek, July 23, 2000, p.46.

29   Hattori, R., Desimaru, M., Nagayama, I. and Inoue, K. (1991) "Autistic and devel-
     opmental disorders after general anaesthetic delivery." *The Lancet 337*, 1357–8.

30   Rhodes, M.C., Seidler, F.J., Abdel-Rahman, A., Tate, C.A., Nyska, A., Rincavag,
     H.L. and Slotkin, T.A. (2004) "Terbutaline is a developmental neurotoxicant:
     Effects on neuroproteins and morphology in cerebellum, hippocampus, and

somatosensory cortex." *Journal of Pharmacology and Experimental Therapeutics 308*, 2, 529–37.

31   Rhodes, M.C., Seidler, F.J., Qiao, D., Tate, C.A., Cousins, M.M. and Slotkin, T.A. (2004) "Does pharmacotherapy for preterm labor sensitize the developing brain to environmental neurotoxicants? Cellular and synaptic effects of sequential exposure to terbutaline and chlorpyrifos in neonatal rats." *Toxicology and Applied Pharmacology 195*, 2, 203–17.

32   Beech, B.L. (1999) "Drugs in labour: What effects do they have 20 years hence?" *Midwifery Today*. Available at www.midwiferytoday.com (accessed 8 October 2007).

33   Cited by Kolata, G.B. in "Behavioral teratology: Birth defects of the mind." *Science 202*, 17, November 1978.

34   Dozor, J. and Baruth, S. (1999) "Drugs in labor: Are they really necessary…or even safe?" *Mothering Magazine*, August. Available at www.mothering.com (accessed 8 October 2007).

35   Wagner, M. (2000) "Technology in birth: First do no harm." *Midwifery Today* . Available at www.midwiferytoday.com (accessed 8 October 2007).

36   Ang, E.S., Jr., Gluncic, V., Duque, A., Schafer, M.E. and Rakic, P. (2006) "Prenatal exposure to ultrasound waves impacts neuronal migration in mice." *Proceedings of the National Academy of Sciences USA 103*, 34, 12903–10. See also: Brownlee, C. (2006) "Bad vibrations? Ultrasound disturbs mouse brains." *Science News 170*, 7, 99.

37   Wagner, M. (2000) "Technology in birth: First do no harm." *Midwifery Today* . Available at www.midwiferytoday.com (accessed 8 October 2007).

38   Webb, D.A. and Culhane, J. (2002) "Time of day variation in rates of obstetric intervention to assist in vaginal delivery." *Journal of Epidemiology and Community Health 56*, 8, 577–8.

39   Crook, W., n.d. "The Effects of Candida on Mental Health." Available at www.alternativementalhealth.com/articles/candida.htm (accessed 27 September 2007).

40   Moore, T.J. (1989) *Prescription for Disaster*. New York: Dell Publishing.

41   Walker, S. (1996) *A Dose of Sanity*. New York: John Wiley & Sons, Inc.

CHAPTER 8

Why NO Dyslogical Child is "Hopeless"

"If you think you can, or think you can't, you're right."

—Henry Ford

So far, I've talked mostly about dyslogical behavior caused by bad diets, toxins, allergens, and other environmental factors. But there are children whose brains don't work right for still other reasons: because these children are genetically impaired, or suffered debilitating head injuries, or have seizure disorders, or were born addicted to cocaine or damaged by alcohol.

You might think that these children are hopeless. Not so!

I can say this with great authority, because for more than 30 years I've been involved in research into one of the most "hopeless" of brain disorders, infantile autism. When I began, nearly all autistic children were institutionalized, and the overwhelming majority remained mentally retarded throughout their lifetimes. Now, three decades later, growing numbers of autistic children are recovering and can live happy and useful lives. Their recovery is brought about through a combination of treatments including intensive educational and nutritional interventions, toxin removal, and sensory therapies. This is occurring even though autism involves strong genetic influences, and despite the fact that brain scans and other tests show that autistic children's brains are different in many ways from non-disabled children's—facts once cited as proof that the disorder was incurable.

If we can help even these most "hopeless" of children, it is clearly foolish to underestimate the potential of other children with other brain impairment. Among this group are children who have learning, behavioral, or emotional problems that don't stem (at least directly) from dysfunctional diets, exposure to toxins, or other damaging influences during childhood. Remarkably, the same interventions that work well for children with environmentally caused dysfunction can lead to equally dramatic changes in children with problems ranging from genetic flaws to head injuries and seizures.

Genes aren't (necessarily) destiny

Many people have a pessimistic attitude about the treatability of disorders, such as schizophrenia or autism, in which genetics play a role. Often, when I sense such an attitude in an audience at one of my lectures, I take on a very solemn demeanor, lean forward toward the microphone, and say, slowly and in a hushed personal voice, "I must tell you that I personally have a genetic problem that, if it were not correctable, would leave me severely handicapped and could make it hard for me to earn a living to support my family."

A shocked, sympathetic hush pervades the auditorium as the audience leans forward attentively to hear more about my problem. After a suitable pause, I slowly take off my glasses and explain, "Don't feel too sorry for me—lots of people are nearsighted."

Like my nearsightedness, behavior and learning are to a large degree controlled by genetics. Genes are a powerful factor in learning disabilities, behavioral problems, and even criminality (see Chapter 3). One study of twins, for instance, compared genetic and non-genetic influences on behavior, and concluded, "Estimates of genetic influences on attention problems (60 to 68 percent), aggression (70 to 77 percent), and anxious/depressed behaviors (61 to 65 percent) were high for both sexes."[1] Other studies reveal similarly strong genetic influences on conduct disorder, bullying, alcoholism, and even compulsive gambling.[2]

Many parents and professionals see this news as upsetting. They erroneously equate "genetic" with "untreatable" or, at best, believe that effective treatments for genetically caused or influenced disorders are only a dream for the future. Fortunately, this pessimistic viewpoint is belied by the facts. Many children with genetically influenced brain impairments can be helped, not in the distant future but *today*. Indeed, it's often easier to ameliorate problems caused by a gene defect than it is to fix other biomedical problems. For example:

- Dyslexia, a reading disability, is strongly influenced by genes. In addition to causing reading problems, dyslexia is linked to an increased risk of substance abuse, delinquency, and criminality, with some recent studies showing that *half or more* of the prison population suffers from dyslexia.[3] Researchers recently reported that "pre-adolescent dyslexic children show a wide range of behavior problems that cannot be attributed to social or developmental background variables."[4]

  We can't yet alter the genes involved in dyslexia, but we can often reduce dyslexic children's academic and behavior problems. For instance, children with dyslexia are among those reported to benefit greatly from fatty acid supplements as seen in the Durham research trials (see Chapter 5). In one early study of dyslexic children, researcher Alexandra Richardson reported, "Particular improvements were found in attention, concentration and working memory, but disruptive behavior and hyperactivity in these children also responded to [the] treatment, and marked reductions were seen in anxiety and withdrawal."[5]

- Children with celiac disease, a condition that prevents them from digesting the gluten in wheat correctly, often suffer from behavioral problems or mood disorders, and some even become psychotic. Research also links problems in digesting gluten or casein (a milk protein) to autism, attention deficit hyperactivity disorder (ADHD), and schizophrenia.

Celiac disease is strongly genetically influenced, and other forms of gluten or casein intolerance also undoubtedly stem in part from genetic vulnerability. Yet a dietary treatment—the removal of gluten and/or casein from the diet, along with supplements of certain digestive enzymes needed to break down foods properly—can result in partial or even complete remission of behavioral symptoms.

Why can we often reduce the problems caused by genetic defects without dealing directly with the genes themselves? Because in many cases, if we can gain insight into how an aberrant, missing, or duplicated gene disturbs metabolism or development, we can correct the problem "downstream." We do this, for instance, when we treat children with the genetic disorder phenylketonuria (PKU). If you're a parent, the hospital probably tested your child for PKU soon after birth. That's because individuals with PKU can't metabolize the amino acid phenylalanine correctly, and will become mentally retarded and develop seizures if they eat ordinary food. If started on a special low-phenylalanine diet immediately after birth, however, these infants develop normally, as long as their blood phenylalanine levels stay low for the rest of their lives.

In PKU, a cognitive and behavioral defect that stems from a genetic defect can be controlled entirely by a proper nutritional regimen. Such cases, moreover, are far from rare. Children born with defects in vitamin B12 metabolism often will, if left untreated, develop serious cognitive problems by early adulthood (and some will become brain-damaged in infancy), but prompt detection and treatment may reduce or prevent these problems. Anemias due to folic acid or iron deficiency, also often genetically influenced, can cause learning and behavior problems, and can be completely controlled by proper nutrition. So can a particular form of seizures caused by an inborn defect in the ability to utilize vitamin B6.

While many genes influence the body's ability to use nutrients, others (such as the defect that causes PKU) cause harm by disrupting the metabolism of normally beneficial substances. Still other genes make some of us more susceptible to the ravages of chemicals and heavy metals than others. For instance, at least three different genes may influence how susceptible a child is to lead poisoning,[6] and new research indicates that at least two maternal genes influence the effects of prenatal tobacco exposure on unborn children.[7] Moreover, children's bodies have different abilities to use nutrients such as vitamin C and the B vitamins, which can help the body undo the damage that toxins cause (see Chapter 5).

This is one reason we should welcome rather than fear research on genes and behavior. Identifying genetic vulnerabilities in today's troubled children will allow us, some day, to reduce rates of learning disabilities and even criminality by protecting children from the toxins, nutrient deficiencies, or other environmental insults that could make their brains dyslogical. And even today, we can often treat the problems that faulty genes cause—in many cases with dramatic results.

The child who arrived in Dr. William Walsh's office one day was most doctors' nightmare: a violent, vicious, biting, scratching, swearing terror. At three, Jack (not his real name) had killed his hamster. At four, he'd killed the family cat just to see how loud it would cry. His mom told Dr. Walsh, "He didn't even think he'd done anything wrong."

At five, Jack tried to kill himself by hanging himself from a swing set, cutting his throat with a knife, and jumping from a moving car. At six, his school expelled him. Around that time, he hit his sister so hard with a brick that she needed to be hospitalized. Physicians didn't offer Jack's mother any help. Instead, they told her that it must be her fault: that she and her husband were bad parents, that they had a dysfunctional home.

Just as they'd reached the end of their rope and decided to institutionalize their child so he couldn't injure or kill his siblings, Jack's parents learned about the Pfeiffer Treatment Center in Illinois. The center, directed by Dr. Walsh, uses extensive and sophisticated tests to identify metal imbalances and related metabolic abnormalities in violent, learning-disabled, and troubled children.

Jack's mother immediately called the center for an appointment, and braved a harrowing plane trip with her out-of-control child in order to get there. Her tenacity, Dr. Walsh says, paid off. At the center, tests showed that Jack suffered from a genetic metal imbalance problem. The center's staff designed a tailor-made treatment plan for him, including specially formulated nutritional supplements, to restore his system to normality.

Within ten months, Dr. Walsh reports, the boy was a different person. By the time he was eight, he was a Tiger Scout. He went back to school, and eventually was placed in a gifted program. He became normal, happy, and healthy. When he got into trouble, he did "kid stuff," such as calling his sister fat, or making fun of his brother's mustache—not chasing the family with a butcher knife, or threatening to kill himself.

Jack, the little boy in the case study above, was a psychopath: a person with no conscience, no moral sense, and no empathy for the suffering of others. Psychopaths are considered incurable, and while they make up only about five percent of the general population, they constitute twenty percent of the prison population. They're the Charles Mansons, Ted Bundys, or Albert Shawcrosses—hideous monsters who've been born, apparently, without souls.

Yet William Walsh, the senior scientist at the Pfeiffer Center where this child was treated, says that the majority of kids with psychopathic behaviors can become happy, loving children if they receive the right treatment. In fact, he says, "They're our favorites." What makes Walsh succeed in most cases, when nearly everyone else fails—virtually 100 percent of the time—to turn psychopaths into decent human beings? He doesn't psychoanalyze them, or punish them, or school them. Instead, he detoxifies them.

Walsh has identified one type of genetic culprit in particular that can make children like Jack crazy. The defect involves a gene or genes coding for the production of metallothioneins, a group of proteins the body uses to detoxify heavy metals. Walsh's preliminary research links metallothionein defects and resulting metal imbalances to a large percentage of cases of psychopathic and violent behavior, a finding that his research with some of the world's worst killers bears out. Charles Manson, serial killer Henry Lee Lucas, and "postal rage" killer Patrick Sherril, for instance, all proved to have marked metal imbalances.

When children genetically vulnerable to heavy metals are tested, Walsh and his colleagues identify different patterns of metal imbalance, with abnormally low levels of some metals being as problematic as abnormally high levels of others. Using the information from an exhaustive body of tests, the Pfeiffer Center designs a program of nutritional therapy that flushes dangerous metals from the system, elevates levels of metals that are too low, and restores normal brain functioning.

The majority of children the Pfeiffer Center treats for abnormal heavy metal metabolism or other biochemical defects show striking reductions in violent behavior, with one study of 207 consecutive patients who complied with treatment showing that 92 percent markedly reduced their assaultive behavior, with 58 percent ceasing their violent behavior altogether.[8] What's most remarkable, again, is that many of these are children labeled as psychopaths and sociopaths, whom the textbooks have long reported to be incurable.

Walsh's work is a prime example of why people who fear research into the genetics of violence and criminality, and those who believe that all children are born "clean slates" who become dysfunctional only because of a poor upbringing, are dead wrong. Jack wouldn't have benefited from years of sociological or psychological intervention, because the circuitry of his metal-laden brain couldn't understand logic or even love. Now, with his genetic vulnerability detected and his brain health restored by corrective treatment, he doesn't need counseling or psychotherapy, because he can respond to the nurturing experiences of everyday life that have been there all along.

Fixing the "broken" brain

Another group of children particularly likely to be labeled as incurable are those who've experienced serious brain injuries. Children who suffer drastic brain damage, as a result of accidents, carbon monoxide poisoning, or other trauma, generally receive grim prognoses from their doctors. Most are at high risk for aberrant behavior, depression, hyperactivity, learning disabilities, and a host of other problems. Yet here again, nutritional therapies can sometimes lead to partial or even full recoveries.

I first learned about this seemingly impossible occurrence from Carlton Fredericks, Ph.D., who treated many such patients at the Atkins Center for Alternative Therapies in New York. "I have had as dinner guests in my home patients, brain damaged by carbon monoxide, oxygen deprivation, and trauma, for whom the original prognosis was 'chronic vegetative state,'" he told me. His treatment: octacosanol, a fatty acid derived from wheat germ oil and also found in other vegetable waxes and oils.

This, of course, is the sort of treatment that traditional doctors like to mock: "Mrs. Smith, do you really think you can reverse brain damage with *wheat germ oil?*" But Fredericks' clinical observations suggested that octacosanol indeed "is capable of stimulating the repair of damaged neurons, even in the brain, where such repair is classically described as unachievable." And while doctors continue to dismiss octacosanol cures as "spontaneous" remissions, the stories of Fredericks' patients clearly show that octacosanol treatment works—often within weeks—when all other treatments fail.

Patricia Kane believes in octacosanol, because she saw it work. When her two-year-old son Shawn fell from a slide onto cement and became comatose, doctors said Shawn was hopelessly brain-damaged, and would spend the rest of his life in a vegetative state.

Refusing to accept this prognosis, Kane contacted Dr. Fredericks, who recommended giving Shawn a broad spectrum of nutrients. For two weeks, Kane saw no progress. Doctors moved Shawn to the hospital's rehabilitation center, in preparation to finding an institution for him. But before they could do so, Shawn amazed them by standing—and then running. (His doctor, Kane says, "stomped off in a huff" when Shawn defied his prognosis; later he credited physical therapy, although Shawn had received none.)

"Every day that passed," Kane says, "Shawn got better. I continued his nutrient program vigorously—much to the distress of the nurses, who lectured me on the dangers of vitamins." Within a few weeks, Shawn was cured, except for a slight limp. Doctors continued to credit his miraculous turnaround to the physical therapy he'd never received, but admitted that they'd never seen such an astonishing recovery.

Kane learned the specific reason for that recovery when, while visiting California, she ran out of the wheat-germ-oil concentrate that she'd been giving Shawn. He began to limp, and then to fall, regressing before her eyes. "I did not see the connection," she says, "until we retuned home (at once) and I purchased more of the supplement." In one week, all of Shawn's symptoms had disappeared again.

From that point on, Shawn continued to take the wheat germ oil, and he continued to thrive. By the age of 17, he'd graduated from high school ahead of time, and had become a gifted artist. Says Kane, who now counsels parents in similar situations, "'Hopeless' occurs to many different degrees in many different health problems children experience. But it doesn't have to be accepted." [9]

Shawn is just one of dozens of brain-injured children who have made remarkable recoveries from so-called "permanent" brain injuries, after receiving octacosanol treatment. If Shawn and many other children can recover from devastating head injuries, there should be even greater hope for children with dyslogic stemming from lesser injuries. And there are more of such children than you might think: growing research links even relatively mild head injuries, such as concussions, to an increased risk for hyperactivity, conduct disorder, and psychosocial deficits. [10]

Why do nutritional supplements like octacosanol help many children with head injuries that seemingly have nothing to do with diet? A head injury, in addition to causing physical damage, disrupts the biochemistry of the brain. To restore its integrity, the brain needs a good supply of the proper building blocks of cells and neuro-transmitters: essential fatty acids, vitamins, minerals, and other nutrients. An injured brain that is well supplied with these nutrients has a fighting chance, while a brain lacking in these raw materials is probably doomed to long-term or even permanent dysfunction.

FAS: can some of the damage be undone?

Earlier, I talked about the tragedy of Fetal Alcohol Syndrome (FAS) and the less-severe but still crippling Fetal Alcohol Effects (FAE). Children born damaged by prenatal alcohol exposure suffer from serious learning and behavioral problems, and many become delinquents or criminals. Even for these children, however, a nutritional therapy can offer hope—in spite of the fact that their brains are wounded well before birth.

Recently, Jennifer Thomas and colleagues tested the effects of the B vitamin choline on the learning and memory of rat pups exposed to alcohol before birth. One group of alcohol-exposed rat pups received choline, another received a placebo, and a third group received no intervention. The researchers also evaluated two groups of non-alcohol-exposed rats.

Testing the learning ability of all of the rats soon after birth, the researchers found that the alcohol-exposed rats not given choline made numerous errors. Those given choline, however, performed as well as the alcohol-free rats on a test of visual discrimination and memory. Additional analysis showed that the benefits of choline stemmed not from immediate effects of the nutrient, but from long-term changes that the nutrient caused in the rats' brains. "Impor-tantly," the researchers say, "choline treatment was effective in reducing the severity of fetal alcohol effects even when treatment occurred after the alcohol exposure period."[11]

In a 2006 study, researchers at Cornell conducted a similar study of mice exposed to alcohol during a period corresponding to late human fetal development. The exposed mice were hyperactive, had trouble learning and remembering, and weren't fearful when they should be—much like children with FAS. But when the mice received nicotinamide, a form of vitamin B3, immediately after alcohol exposure, they looked just like non-exposed mice. "To our knowledge," the researchers said, "this is the first treatment that has been shown to work at the molecular, cellular, and behavioral levels."[12]

This doesn't mean, of course, that it's safe to drink during pregnancy, or that FAS and FAE can be "fixed" after birth. But it means that doctors who identify FAS in a child at birth or shortly afterward may be able to partially reverse the damage that prenatal alcohol exposure has caused. And even a small improvement in a child with alcohol-caused impairment can make a big difference—perhaps the difference between a happy, productive life in the community, and a life on the streets or in prison.

Treating epilepsy with diet

Epilepsy, in addition to its physical effects, often causes behavior and learning problems. Doctors once attributed these problems to the embarrassment and stigmatization that children with epilepsy suffer, but two recent studies reveal that even before seizures are detected— and, thus, before any stigma or embarrassment exists—children with epilepsy exhibit abnormal anxiety, depression, attention deficits, and behavior problems.[13] In addition, temporal lobe epilepsy can be associated with senseless acts of rage or violence.

While doctors label most cases of epilepsy as "idiopathic," meaning that they can't pinpoint a cause, the doctors I work with often find causes, including toxic exposure, food allergies, and vaccine injury. However, a number of children develop seizures in the absence of obvious environmental triggers. It's likely that these children, or at least a large percentage of them, have a genetic vulnerability. But even when seizures have little or nothing to do with diet or toxins, nutritional therapy can offer help or in some cases even a cure. Moreover, nutritional approaches are far safer and have fewer side effects than drugs, and often work in cases where drugs are ineffective.

One therapy, called the ketogenic diet, is very high in certain fats, low in carbohydrates, and low in protein. Doctors don't know why it works, but it often does. It's effective for young children with a variety

of different seizure types—and while it's not entirely risk-free, it's infinitely safer than the anticonvulsive drugs usually used as a front-line
treatment. The ketogenic diet also improves mood and behavior in
many epileptic children, and a recent Johns Hopkins University study
of 34 children who stayed on the diet for a year found that the
children—in addition to having fewer seizures—showed improvements in attention and social functioning.[14] Started early enough, the
diet can actually stop epilepsy in its tracks in many children, preventing a lifetime of seizures and associated behavior problems.

Once again, this is a case in which a gene-influenced problem can
be treated, and in many cases cured, by a dietary therapy. That therapy,
however, was almost ignored until recently. Doctors at Johns Hopkins
discovered the ketogenic diet's effects decades ago, but the approach
was scorned by physicians who preferred to prescribe anticonvulsants.
(To their credit, Johns Hopkins continued to promote the diet.)

Fortunately, the ketogenic diet is now making a dramatic
comeback in the medical community, with prestigious hospitals now
promoting its use. Much of the credit belongs to several generations of
parents who've discovered the diet on their own, implemented it on
their own (usually in the face of medical opposition), found that it
worked, and spread the word to other patients. Eventually, this "parent
power" pressured the medical community into researching the
ketogenic diet and affirming its benefits.

Autism and schizophrenia: hope for the most "hopeless" of mental disorders

While this book focuses primarily on the types of dyslogic that cause
children to become violent or fail at school and later at life, it's
important to point out that the nutritional and toxin-removing
therapies I've discussed can address even more serious brain dysfunction, including outright psychosis.

As I noted earlier, I first began researching autism more than 40
years ago, at a time when parents were advised to simply institutionalize their autistic children and forget that they existed. The only "treatments" offered at the time were toxic drugs that turned the children
into zombies, or psychotherapy, which focused exclusively on blaming

the mothers of autistic children for subconsciously rejecting their children.

In my effort to find help for my own autistic son and other autistic children, I began communicating with families worldwide. After publishing my book *Infantile Autism* in 1964, I started receiving hundreds of letters from parents of autistic children throughout the United States, including a number who had tried the then-new idea of "megavitamin therapy" on their autistic children. I initially was quite skeptical about the remarkable improvement being reported by some of these parents, but as evidence accumulated, I became increasingly curious. Eventually, I undertook a large-scale study on more than 200 autistic children, giving them megadoses of several nutrients. By the end of the four-month trial, it became clear that at least one of these nutrients—vitamin B6—caused dramatic improvement in many of the children.

Since that time, 21 studies of B6 treatment for autism, by researchers in seven countries, have shown positive results. Other nutrients—including magnesium, omega-3 fatty acids, dimethylglycine (DMG), and thiamine—also benefit many of these children. And thousands of parents report that implementing a gluten-free, casein-free diet, or a diet free of yeast, very often brings about nearly miraculous improvement in their autistic children.

As a result, we currently are seeing a revolution in autism treatment, in which parents in droves are turning away from the only treatment that most doctors routinely offer—the use of psychotropic drugs that merely mask symptoms—and toward the use of natural, safe, effective nutrients and dietary changes. As they do, growing numbers of doctors are beginning to investigate these approaches, at first with reluctance and skepticism and then with increasing enthusiasm when they discover that these treatments work. When the Autism Research Institute began its Defeat Autism Now! (DAN!) conferences in 1996 to promote orthomolecular approaches to treating autism, a handful of professionals attended. Now, a few years later, our conferences are "standing room only," with doctors from all over the world participating. Many of these doctors are themselves parents of autistic children who found conventional medicine ineffective, in contrast to the remarkable improvement achieved in their own and other autistic children using orthomolecular approaches.[15]

The treatment of schizophrenia is following, albeit more slowly, a similar path. In the 1950s, doctors blamed schizophrenia on bad parents, the disease was considered incurable in most cases, and the only available treatment was psychoanalysis. When psychotherapy proved to be a colossal failure, physicians simply turned to drugging schizophrenics—an approach that allows a minority to function more or less normally, but offers only limited help for many others and no help at all for as many as a third of schizophrenics. Today, most physicians still consider the use of psychotropic drugs to be "state of the art" treatment for schizophrenia, but a growing number—led by pioneering physician Abram Hoffer, M.D., Ph.D., who has successfully treated schizophrenia with non-drug therapies for decades—are offering an alternative: safe and effective orthomolecular treatments that work for many patients labeled as hopeless.

In 1995, "JM" walked into the office of Abram Hoffer, M.D. She'd been mentally disturbed since the age of 14, fearing that her best friends were aliens and that she was being stalked by a shadowy man. As a teenager, she began savagely hitting her head and body, and cutting her arms. By the age of 20, she'd withdrawn from work and friends, convinced that she had two brains, that she sometimes became invisible, and that her body parts were becoming detached.

Doctors put JM on drugs. They diagnosed her, at various times, as having adjustment disorder, post traumatic stress disorder, and borderline personality disorder. They blamed presumptive inadequate parenting and presumptive early sexual abuse, even though JM denied both of these allegations. One doctor told her that getting a job would cure her. It didn't: her hallucinations, depression, delusions, confusion, and disorientation grew increasingly worse.

Then a friend told JM about Dr. Hoffer, a physician specializing in treating psychiatric disorders with orthomolecular therapies. Hoffer saw JM, and diagnosed her as schizophrenic. Immediately,

*he started her on high-dose supplements of niacin, a therapy that
Hoffer and his colleagues have used successfully to treat hundreds of
"incurable" schizophrenics. She also received additional nutrients,
followed a sugar-free diet, and underwent an elimination diet to
identify food sensitivities. After two weeks, she felt so good that she
discontinued the treatment, thinking she was cured—only to relapse
quickly. She re-started the supplements and diet, and did not suffer
another schizophrenic episode during the next year except on two
occasions when she ate chocolate (a food to which she is sensitive,
according to Hoffer's tests) and one occasion when she had the flu.*

*"I am, for the first time since my preteens, relaxed, calm, stable
and energetic," JM commented in a medical journal article.[16] "I am
able to concentrate, converse, and read without a 'second brain's'
interference." She adds, "I am certain of what has treated me. It is
both the elimination of allergens [and] the vitamins themselves....I
know orthomolecular treatment to be essential not only in providing
effective remedy to various forms of disease, but in rekindling hope,
focus and determination where there may be none."*

*Says Hoffer of his patient, "It is likely that had she not started on
the orthomolecular regimen, she would have spent the rest of her life
in and out of institutions, or in and out of the streets, until she would
have died by suicide, by exhaustion, or by homicide." Instead, with a
few pennies' worth of nutrients, she is well.*

Working hand-in-hand: biology, education, and other treatments

Dyslogic is a biological problem, not an educational one. Nevertheless,
some educational approaches—while they won't cure dyslogic—can
greatly alleviate some of its most frustrating symptoms.

Of all of the psychological therapies tried with dyslogic, the only
one proven to be effective, in many cases, is behavior modification or
"applied behavior analysis." (A related therapy, called cognitive behavioral therapy or CBT, can also be useful with children whose

dyslogical behaviors are minor.) Perhaps the most important aspect of behavior modification is the concentration upon specific, observable, countable behaviors. Unlike previous methods, there are no assumptions made about hypothetical emotional blocks, concealed conflicts, or covert hostilities which must be "worked out" or "understood." Instead, on the assumption that the child has a deficiency in his behavior repertoire, new behaviors are systematically built in a series of carefully planned and rewarded small steps.

Basically, behavior modification teaches appropriate behaviors by rewarding them, and discourages inappropriate behaviors by ignoring them or exacting consequences. For instance, a dyslogical child who refrains from fighting for an entire day might get a toy or special privileges, while a dyslogical child caught stealing money from his parents might be required to do several hours of extra work for them. It sounds almost too simple to work, but in fact it is one of the most powerful behavior-changing tools ever developed—safer and more powerful than drugs, and certainly more powerful than psychotherapy. Similarly, CBT, which focuses on practical, here-and-now skills that can help dyslogical people cope with their problems, can often improve behavior dramatically.

While behavior modification and cognitive behavioral therapy can help, however, they can't cure. Behavior modification may reduce the aberrant behaviors of someone with dyslogic, but it won't change the underlying cause of his dyslogic. All educational programs—even the best ones—are imperfect solutions for disorders that are not educational but biological. Finding a good educational program is important, but it is more important to attack dyslogic at its roots, with treatments that address its causes rather than just reducing its symptoms.

These treatments include the dietary and toxin-removing approaches I've described, but they also include other biological approaches. I know researchers who are having remarkable success with everything from neurofeedback to sensory stimulation to computerized "brain retraining" programs. And while the first rule of treatment is "earlier is better," the second is "it might not ever be too late." Kenneth Stoller recently reported that, when he treated a boy with FAS using hyperbaric oxygen therapy, the boy showed astonishing improvements—even though he was 15 years old at the time of treatment. Says Stoller, "It is time to revise the old concept that brain injury is a condition for which there is no treatment other than supportive measures."[17]

In the future, our treatment options will expand even further. They will include stem cell therapy, already showing promise as a way to restore brain cells damaged or destroyed by disease or toxins. And they will include personalized DNA profiles, allowing us to detect our children's genetic vulnerabilities and address them before cognitive or behavioral problems occur.

The heartening message to take from all of this, if you are a parent dealing with a dyslogical child, is that your child is not "hopeless." It's a virtual certainty that your child can be helped and possibly even be cured—no matter what the cause of your child's problem, and no matter how many doctors have told you to give up. There are treatments available now, and additional treatments on the horizon, that have the power to effectively address nearly any form of brain dysfunction. To discover them, however, you must look beyond traditional medicine, which has relied for decades on psychoanalyzing or drugging dyslogical children, and seek real treatments that make the body, and the brain, whole and healthy.

Notes

1   Hudziak, J.J., Rudiger, L.P., Neale, M.C., Heath, A.C. and Todd, R.D. (2000) "A twin study of inattentive, aggressive, and anxious/depressed behaviors." *Journal of the American Academy of Child and Adolescent Psychiatry 39*, 469–76.

2   "Gene research highlights." *Crime Times* 2001, 7, 4, 7.

3   Kirk, J. and Reid, G. (2001) "An examination of the relationship between dyslexia and offending in young people and the implications for the training system." *Dyslexia 7*, 2, 77–84; and Santiago, H.C. (1995) "Visual and educational dysfunctions in a group of Hispanic residents of a juvenile detention center." Presentation to the American Academy of Optometry.

4   Heiervang, E., Stevenson, J., Lund, A. and Hugdahl, K. (2001) "Behaviour problems in children with dyslexia." *Nordic Journal of Psychiatry 55*, 4, 251–6.

5   Richardson, A. (2001) "Fatty acids in dyslexia, dyspraxia, ADHD and the autistic spectrum.," *Nutrition Practitioner 3*, 3, 18–24.

6   Onalaja, A.O. and Claudio, L. (2000) "Genetic susceptibility to lead poisoning."
    Environmental Health Perspectives 108, S1, 23–8.

7   Hong, Y.C., Lee, K.H., Son, B.K., Ha, E.H., Moon, H.S. and Ha, M. (2003)
    "Effects of the GSTM1 and GSTT1 polymorphisms on the relationship between
    maternal exposure to environmental tobacco smoke and neonatal birth weight."
    Journal of Occupational and Environmental Medicine 45, 5, 492–8.

8   Walsh, W.J., Glab, L.B. and Haakenson, M.L. (2004) "Reduced violent behavior
    following biochemical therapy." *Physiology and Behavior 82*, 5, 835–9.

9   Kane, P. (1985) *Food Makes the Difference*. New York: Simon and Schuster.

10 McKinlay, A., Dalrymple-Alford, J.C., Horwood, L.J. and Fergusson, D.M. (2002)
    "Long term psychosocial outcomes after mild head injury in early childhood."
    Journal of Neurology, Neurosurgery, and Psychiatry 73, 3, 281–8.

11 Thomas, J.D., La Fiette, M.H., Quinn, V.R. and Riley, E.P. (2000) "Neonatal
    choline supplementation ameliorates the effects of prenatal alcohol exposure on a
    discrimination learning task in rats." *Neurotoxicology and Teratology 22*, 5, 703–11.

12 Ieraci, A. and Herrera, D. (2006) "Nicotinamide protects against ethanol-induced
    apoptotic neurodegeneration in the developing mouse brain." *PLoS Medicine 3*, 4.
    Available at http://medicine.plosjournals.org/perlserv/?request=get-document%
    doi=10.1371/journal.pmed.0030101&ct=1 (accessed 27 September 2007).

13 Dunn, D.W., Harezlak, J., Ambrosius, W.T., Austin, J.K. and Hale, B. (2002)
    "Teacher assessment of behaviour in children with new-onset seizures." *Seizure 11*,
    3, 169–75; and Austin, J.K., Harezlak, J., Dunn, D.W., Huster, G.A., Rose, D.F.
    and Ambrosius, W.T. (2001) "Behavior problems in children before first recog-
    nized seizures." *Pediatrics 107*, 1, 115–22.

14 Pulsifer, M.B., Gordon, J.M., Brandt, J., Vining, E.P. and Freeman, J.M. (2001)
    "Effects of ketogenic diet on development and behavior: Preliminary report of a
    prospective study." *Developmental Medicine and Child Neurology 43*, 5, 301–6.

15 See *Physicians who have successfully treated their own autistic children: The Defeat Autism
    Now! (DAN!) Doctors* (videotapes, July 2001 [Part 1] and July 2002 [Part 2]).

16 Hoffer, A. and "Ms. JM" (pseudonym) (1996) Inside schizophrenia: Before and
    after treatment. *Journal of Orthomolecular Medicine 11*, 1. Available at
    www.healthy.net/scr/Article.asp?Id=708 (accessed 27 September 2007).

17 Stoller, K. (2005) "Quantification of neurocognitive changes before, during and
    after hyperbaric oxygen therapy in a case of fetal alcohol syndrome." *Pediatrics
    116*, 4, e586–91.

CHAPTER 9

An Action Plan
for Ending Dyslogic

"Every individual has the ability to make the world a much better place, in big or small ways, for the next generation."

—Stephen M. Edelson, Director, Autism Research Institute

The readers of this book come from many walks of life, and view the problem of dyslogic from many different vantage points. Many of you are parents, coping with the day-to-day disasters that occur in the lives of dyslogical children, and fearing for your children's future. Others of you are teachers, trying to impart knowledge to students who can't learn, can't obey rules, can't sit still, and sometimes even make you fear for your own safety. Some of you are doctors, besieged by desperate parents looking for help. And some of you are judges, legislators, parole officers, and counselors looking for ways to help troubled children whose dyslogic drives them to commit foolish or horrific acts.

As you witness the ravages of dyslogic from these different viewpoints, all of you have two overriding concerns: how to help dyslogical children turn their lives around, and how to prevent the devastating effects of brain dysfunction in future generations. The message of this book is that *these problems can be solved*. To succeed, however, all of the people involved in the lives of dyslogical children—parents, teachers, counselors, doctors, judges, parole officers—must do their part.

In this chapter, I outline the basics of a plan to attack dyslogic on every front: the home, the school, the doctor's office, and even the courtroom and the jail. To some of you, this plan may seem like a pipe dream—but it is already being implemented by growing numbers of parents and professionals. More importantly, *wherever it is implemented, it works!*

There is no time like now to join the people who say "no" to failed drug and psychotherapy treatments, and "no" to the idea that dyslogical children are doomed to lives of failure. And there is no time like now to say "yes" to the idea that every dyslogical child can be helped, and many dyslogical children can be cured. Every day, dyslogical children are being lost in the system; but every day, as well, other dyslogical children are being saved by parents and professionals willing to replace failed strategies with approaches that work. Here are these strategies, summarized in an "action plan" for parents and professionals.

Action plan for parents

The first step in this plan, if you are a parent dealing with a troubled, violent, or delinquent child, is simply this: stop feeling guilty.

As I noted in the introduction to this book, parents of autistic and schizophrenic children were paralyzed by misplaced guilt, heaped on them by "experts" who claimed at the time that all dysfunctional behavior stemmed from bad parenting. When these parents began to come forward and say, "You are wrong—we love our child, and something else is to blame for this problem," they took the first huge step toward real hope and real treatment for their sons and daughters. We now know that autism, schizophrenia, obsessive-compulsive disorder, and other psychiatric problems stem from problems in the brain, not problems in the home or school or community. But we'd still be treating autistic children by letting them smash clay models of their mothers—a treatment of choice when my autistic son was diagnosed—if parents hadn't said, "Nonsense!"

The same revolution needs to occur in the treatment of dyslogic, and it needs to start with parents. The scientific evidence, as I've outlined it in this book, is clear: you didn't make your son a delinquent by being too strict—or not strict enough—about his homework. You didn't make your daughter a drug addict by missing her soccer games, or refusing to let her dye her hair pink. You didn't make your child dyslogical by being too strict, too lax, too religious, not religious enough, too "stuffy," too relaxed, too protective, or not protective enough.

Your dyslogical child has a physical problem—a *medical* problem. It may stem from toxic exposure, a diet lacking in nutrients, a genetic vulnerability, an infectious process, an undetected seizure disorder, a head injury, a medication reaction, an allergy or food sensitivity, or another condition that affects brain function. No matter which of these problems afflicts your son or daughter, you cannot psychoanalyze it away, and you cannot drug it away. Talk therapy doesn't address a biological problem, and drugs merely mask symptoms while adding toxic chemicals to an already dysfunctional system.

Once you free yourself and your child from failed approaches based on blaming parents or society, you will empower yourself to find therapies that work. Two of these, which are beyond the scope of this book but deserve a mention here, are behavior modification and cognitive behavioral therapy (for a brief discussion, see Chapter 8). Neither of these therapies will cure dyslogic, but both can help you and your child find ways of identifying and controlling—at least to some degree—dyslogical thought patterns. These techniques won't make the brain dysfunction that underlies dyslexia go away, but they can often make life easier for the dyslexic child. Similarly, behavior modification and cognitive therapy can sometimes teach a dyslogical child techniques for "working around" a brain dysfunction that affects thinking and behavior.

In the end, however, the only effective way to address the biological problems that cause dyslogical behavior is to identify and treat their root causes. To do this, you may need medical help—but you probably won't find that help simply by picking a pediatrician from your managed care plan.

That's because, as I've explained, far too many doctors believe that treating dyslogic simply means drugging dyslogical children. Pick any 20 pediatricians at random, and you'll probably find that 19 of them will merely recommend giving your dyslogical child Ritalin, Adderall, Risperdal, or a similar drug. What's worse, they'll make that recommendation after only the most cursory of physical evaluations, and they'll probably scoff at any suggestion that toxins, dietary deficiencies, food sensitivities, infections, metabolic defects, or related causes of dyslogical behavior should be explored.

This is gross medical negligence, because drugs—they may be necessary in some cases—should always be a last, not a first, resort. It is infinitely better to address the root causes of dyslogic than to merely reduce its symptoms with dangerous drugs.

Given this, what should your next step be? I recommend assertively seeking out open-minded doctors who are more interested in natural cures and preventive measures than in masking your child's problem with drugs. You can find such doctors by asking friends and relatives for referrals, by searching on the Internet for doctors who describe themselves as "holistic" or "naturopathic," or by contacting associations such as the American Association of Naturopathic Physicians, the American Holistic Medical Association, and the American Academy of Environmental Medicine. My own institute, the Autism Research Institute, also maintains a list of doctors who focus on safe and natural treatments for children with brain dysfunction. In addition, you can use Internet resources to search for doctors in your area who have published journal articles advocating safe, natural treatments for dyslogical behavior. If your child is extremely violent, I recommend contacting the Pfeiffer Center in Illinois, which has an amazing track record of curing "incurably" aggressive, dangerous, and even psychopathic children.

One more word about seeking medical help: beware of school officials who push you toward doctors bent on prescribing Ritalin or other drugs. Schools have far exceeded their bounds in encouraging—and even harassing—parents to seek drug treatments for children labeled as hyperactive or oppositional. Remember that teachers and counselors are not medical professionals, cannot make medical diagnoses, and have no authority to force you to seek a particular treatment or therapy. (See my action plan for teachers and school officials, later in this chapter, for more on this.)

While you're seeking good medical help, you can take other actions at the same time. Begin with these steps:

- Reduce your use of toxins such as herbicides, pesticides, solvents, and cleaning products. Buy "green" products when you can.

- Get the junk out of your child's diet. Replace sodas with bottled water or juice, making sure it's real juice and not the kind that's mostly sugar water. Replace doughnuts, fast-food meals, and heavily processed canned foods with natural foods you cook yourself. (Yes, your child will object at first, perhaps noisily. But it's worth the struggle.)

- As extra insurance, give your child a good vitamin/mineral supplement each day, along with omega-3 fatty acids.

- Make sure your child gets at least 20 minutes of physical exercise daily, because exercise generates natural "feel-good" substances and can improve behavior dramatically.

- Get rid of moldy or mildewed rugs or tiles, because molds and mildew can make many kids spacey or "crazy."

- Cut down on your child's TV and video-game time and replace it with outdoor play time, because natural sunlight—overly vilified these days—is necessary, at least in small amounts, for mental and physical health. While you're at it, replace your indoor lights with more natural full-spectrum lights.

- Buy filters for your tap water to remove toxins, or use bottled water.

- Become an expert on the pros and cons of childhood vaccinations. If any vaccines containing thimerosal (a mercury-laden preservative—see Chapter 7) are still allowed in your state at the time that you read this book, avoid them! Whenever possible, have your doctor order titers before immunizations, to see if shots are unnecessary. Ask for single-vaccine shots, rather than shots such as measles–mumps–rubella (MMR) that combine several vaccines in potentially dangerous "cocktails." Decide for yourself which vaccines are necessary and which aren't, and stand by your guns—even if it means battling schools and doctors. Before any vaccinations, give your child megadoses of vitamins, particularly A and C. And never, ever allow your doctor to give your child a vaccination if the child is ill. Also, avoid giving a child a repeat dose of a vaccine that previously caused a bad reaction.

Once you've taken these first steps toward combating your child's dyslogic, a good doctor will be able to steer you toward valuable treatments that have helped or even cured tens of thousands of dyslogical children. These may include—to name just a few—therapies to remove heavy metals and other toxins; diets that address nutrient deficiencies, allergies, or food sensitivities; yeast-free, or gluten-free and casein-free, diets; and individually tailored regimens of megadose nutrients to correct deficiencies. It may take some trial and error (as well as a number of laboratory tests) to find the approaches that benefit your child, but the results, more often than not, are remarkable.

It's my experience, in fact, that virtually every dyslogical child whose parents implement such approaches under good medical guidance gets better. Many of them improve so much that people are surprised, later on, to learn that they ever had problems. Others, while not entirely cured, become happier, healthier, more rational, and more loving. And even the minority who remain very troubled often improve to the point where it is infinitely less stressful, and less dangerous, to deal with their behavior. Very, very few fail to benefit significantly, so it is well worth your time and effort to take these steps.

Bear in mind, however, that in being a strong advocate for your child, you will sometimes anger doctors, school counselors, and others in positions of authority. So be it! For far too long, parents have kowtowed to doctors and school officials who insist that their children need dangerous psychotropic drugs, or to counselors and psychiatrists dishing out undeserved blame. It takes a strong parent to resist these pressures, but you must if you wish to find true help and effective treatment for your child.

SUMMARY: ACTION PLAN FOR PARENTS

- Find a doctor trained in natural, preventive medicine. Avoid doctors who recommend drugs (unless you've exhausted all other possibilities) or psychotherapy.

- Clean up your child's environment: water, air, soil. Avoid pesticides and other dangerous household chemicals.

- Provide your child's brain with the right "building blocks" by cutting out junk foods and replacing them with healthful foods and dietary supplements.

- Make sure your child gets enough exercise and exposure to natural sunlight.

- Provide a dyslogical child with supplemental behavior modification or cognitive therapy, which can offer useful strategies for dealing with life problems.

- If you become pregnant, avoid toxins, eat a healthful diet, and avoid unnecessary medical procedures that could harm your child before or during delivery.

A word about prevention....

It is far easier to prevent dyslogic in the first place than it is to correct brain dysfunction once it's already causing dyslogical behavior. Thus, if you're planning on having additional children, it's critical to protect their brains even before their birth. This includes reading up on prenatal nutrition, and possibly consulting a nutrition expert about proper prenatal diet; taking prenatal nutritional supplements; avoiding drugs, tobacco, and alcohol during pregnancy; avoiding exposure to other toxins, such as paints, solvents, and pesticides; saying "no" to ultrasound testing unless there is a good reason for the procedure; and selecting a doctor who opposes the use (except when absolutely necessary) of Cesarean sections, labor-inducing drugs, and other unnatural delivery procedures. If your pregnancy is uncomplicated, you may also want to look into the possibility of using a midwife. And

168 DYSLOGIC SYNDROME

if you're a pregnant or nursing mom, avoid exposure to toxins in the workplace, even if it means finding another job. As my friend Harold Buttram, M.D., notes, "Children are ten times more vulnerable to these chemicals than adults, but a fetus may be 100 more times vulnerable to their effects on brain development"—so don't take chances with your unborn baby's brain.[1]

Action plan for teachers and school officials

Dyslogical kids wreak havoc on a classroom. They disrupt the most carefully planned lessons, drive other children (and sometimes teachers) to tears, and, at worst, threaten the safety of a school's students and staff. It's no wonder that teachers, principals, and school counselors are desperate for solutions that will keep dyslogical children calm, attentive, and obedient.

Unfortunately, the solution that too many schools buy into is to promote the wide-scale drugging of children with Ritalin, Adderall, antidepressants, and other psychotropic medications. Often, these drugs do calm children down. They do so, however, at tremendous cost. Ask kids how drugs make them feel, and many reply, "I feel wired." "I feel zonked." "I don't feel like myself." Moreover, as I noted in Chapter 4, these drugs come with a long-term price tag: they can cause health problems ranging from elevated cancer risk to an increased risk of sudden death from cardiac arrest. And drugs don't cure; they only reduce symptoms, without treating the brain dysfunction that causes them. That's why hyperactive, depressed, oppositional, or antisocial kids are likely to have poor outcomes as adults, even after years of drug therapy intended to make their brains more "normal."

Sadly, far too many schools fail to recognize the poor track record of behavioral drugs in treating behavioral problems, and the pressure that some of these schools place on parents to drug their children is intense. In addition to violating the rights of parents, such pressure doesn't help troubled kids or their families—and in the long run it's not helping schools. As our review of the drug histories of notorious school shooters and other violent kids in Chapter 4 shows, drugging children with Prozac, Ritalin, Adderall, and similar drugs doesn't make schools any safer and in fact may trigger violent outbursts in vulnerable children.

But if drugs aren't the best solution, and "crazy" kids keep other students from learning and frustrate or frighten teachers, what are school officials to do? The answer, as I outlined in Chapter 5, starts with correcting students' body chemistry—not with toxic drugs, but with healthy food that will nourish their starving brains. In that chapter, I described how Appleton Central Alternative High School in Wisconsin, once known for its rude, out-of-control students, and a rate of serious infractions so high that the school required a full-time police officer, now has virtually no problems more major than tardiness or parking violations. How did they do it? The one major change made at the school was the removal of all junk food, and the creation of a breakfast and lunch program supplying whole grains, fruits, vegetables, and preservative-, sugar-, and additive-free foods.

This is, of course, not a simple undertaking. Says Appleton area school district superintendent Dr. Thomas Scullen:

> I think you have to take three or four years to really make a full transition for a [large] district. I think if you try to just implement it all at once, without taking a look at the curriculum, working with the parents and the faculty, you run the danger of really trying to sell something that will sell on its own merits given time.[2]

A more challenging issue for schools investigating the idea of providing healthful meals is (no surprise) money. These days, more and more schools enhance their bottom line by allowing fast-food restaurants to take over cafeteria functions, taking money for selling brand-name foods devoid of nutritional value, and replacing fresh-cooked meals with vending-machine junk. Certified clinical nutritionist Carol Simontacchi notes, "Over $750 million annually is spent on vending machine sales alone, bringing huge dollars into the school coffers... Top sellers are soft drinks, coffee, juice and pseudo-juice drinks, candy, chips, pretzels, cookies, and even French fries." Simontacchi tells of one food service director who balked at selling unhealthful soft drinks until sales representatives from the soft drink company offered his school a $200,000 signing bonus and a stipend of $100,000 per year for ten years, plus a commission from drink sales. He took the offer, and after that he couldn't wait to add more vending machines.[3]

With that kind of money on the line, it's tempting for schools to sell out to fast-food providers, and once these companies gain a foothold it's hard to undo the damage. It takes real courage for school administrators to say no to making an easy buck at the expense of students' health, and to stand up to students' initial complaints when burgers and pizza are replaced by salad bars and turkey burgers on whole-grain buns. But that courage pays off handsomely, in the form of less delinquency, less violence, fewer rules violations, less staff turnover due to frustration with unteachable kids, better test scores, and a saner environment overall. Appleton principal LuAnn Coenen told one interviewer recently, "I would rather quit my job than put another pop or candy machine back in the school."[4]

It's not just the Appleton district that's seeing such results. As I noted in Chapter 5, controlled studies conducted in New York City, Great Britain, and elsewhere show conclusively that better school food leads to better-behaved students, better test scores, and a better educational environment. Enid Hohn, director of the nutrition services division of San Diego's Vista Unified School District, says:

> Kids will eat healthier items and you can still make money, and a pox on anybody who says kids are only going to drink soda and eat Flaming Hot Cheetos. In 10 years I believe we will look back and say, "Can you believe we used to sell that junk to our students?"[5]

This message is getting through to more and more schools, many of which are now joining in a program called "Team Nutrition," offered through the United States Department of Agriculture. The program is designed both to improve the nutritional value of meals served in schools, and to teach children how (and why) to eat right. Teachers, counselors, and school administrators who want to help the hyperactive, attention-disordered, learning disabled, and oppositional children in their classrooms can take a major step by joining in this or a similar program, and by contacting school districts such as Appleton to learn from their success.

What else can you do to help dyslogical students and their families—and to create a classroom environment that works for you as

---

SUMMARY: ACTION PLAN FOR EDUCATORS

- To as great a degree as possible, remove junk food from your school menus and replace it with healthy whole grains, fruits, vegetables, lean meats and low-fat dairy products, and foods free of additives, preservatives, sugar, and artificial sweeteners.
- Reduce children's exposure to toxins such as pesticides, molds and mildew, cleansers, and solvents.
- Implement behavior modification procedures to help dyslogical children learn to control their actions.
- Avoid pushing drug treatments, and be supportive of parents who are trying alternative approaches—even if these approaches don't result in instant improvements in children's behavior.
- Don't blame parents for their children's behavior problems, unless you have concrete evidence of abuse or neglect.

---

well? Be aware of potential toxins in your classroom and school—pesticides, solvents, cleansers, mold, or mildew—and see if they can be removed or (in the case of cleansers and pesticides) replaced with less toxic substances. Be supportive of parents using alternative approaches, and consider reading up on these approaches so you will understand the rationale behind them. Be creative in implementing behavior modification procedures that can help dyslogical children learn to control their actions to a greater degree. Provide plenty of opportunities for children to exercise and "blow off steam" physically in positive ways. And above all, stand up for parents who are trying healthful, non-drug approaches to treat their children's behavior problems.

I'm aware that these are big assignments for teachers who are already over-worked, over-stressed, under-funded, and often working in overcrowded classrooms with too few aides. But as the experience of

Appleton shows, implementing dietary changes and other improve-ments can turn a trouble-ridden facility into a model school, where teachers and staffers actually look forward to each day. Appleton is safer, calmer, happier, and more productive as a result of their "cafeteria revolution," and the teachers there spend far more of their days teaching and far less time babysitting or disciplining. While it will require dedication and effort, you may be able to cause the same miracle to occur at your own school. And isn't it worth a try?

Action plan for physicians and other health care professionals

While mainstream treatments continue to hold sway among most doctors treating dyslogical children, the ranks of caring doctors troubled by the failure of these approaches to help dyslogical children are growing at a fast pace. One reason: as rates of learning disabilities and childhood psychiatric disorders spiral upward, more and more physicians become parents of dyslogical children themselves, and they discover first-hand that these treatments are both ineffective and dangerous. Recently I heard almost identical words from two psychia-trists, both of whom had autistic sons, one from Maryland and the other from California: "It is one thing to be looking for a drug in the *Physicians' Desk Reference* for another mother's child. When it is your own child, you see the same words with very different eyes."

An ever-increasing number of these dissatisfied doctors—both those raising dyslogical children themselves, and those disturbed by the few options they have to offer their dyslogical patients—are actively seeking safer and more effective treatments. I personally know dozens of doctors who have made the journey from drug-oriented medicine to health-oriented medicine. It is not an easy journey to make. It requires casting off years of indoctrination. It requires thinking of health and disease as processes involving all of the body's systems, and therefore treating the entire body so these systems can work effectively in concert, rather than simply thinking of patients as "a brain" or "a bladder" or "a pancreas." It involves stepping outside of a specialty, to see patients as whole beings.

In addition, if you are a doctor who decides to undertake this journey, you will almost certainly alienate many of your colleagues ("You can't possibly believe in that quackery, can you?"), and even some patients who come to you expecting a quick prescription for Ritalin or Risperdal. You'll run the risk of punishment by medical "quality assurance" boards determined to enforce the status quo. You will fight even more battles with insurance companies. You'll spend far more time caring for each of your patients, and possibly earn less money.

Moreover, becoming a health-oriented medical professional requires you to invite patients and their families to be active participants in their treatment, rather than passive onlookers. It requires replacing a prescription pad with hours of intensive testing and experimentation, to determine what makes each dyslogical patient "tick" and what is making each one "crazy." And it requires patience, because while drugs provide the illusion of a quick fix, nutritional and detoxification treatments often (although not always) take time, effort, multiple therapies, and a great deal of trial and error.

What's the reward? You'll see hyperactive children become calm and happy when you supply their bodies with the nutrients they're lacking. You'll see tired, angry, confused, pale, violent, or unhealthy children blossom when you identify and remove the allergens that were making them sick. You'll see miraculous changes in "hopeless" children when you resolve the intestinal abnormalities that allow psychoactive peptides from certain foods to poison their brains. You'll see learning disabled children master reading and math after you lower their toxic levels of lead or mercury. And you'll see depressed children laugh again, and dangerous children become loving and kind, when you identify the allergies, food sensitivities, toxic exposure, or nutritional deficiencies that are making their brains malfunction.

The payoff, in short, is simply this: your patients will improve markedly, and they will love you for helping them. Their parents will love you. You will help children no other doctors can help. And, most importantly, you will nearly eliminate from your vocabulary the two words, "no hope." For a dedicated doctor, it doesn't get any better than that.

SUMMARY: ACTION PLAN FOR PHYSICIANS AND OTHER HEALTH CARE PROFESSIONALS

- Assume that every dyslogical child can be treated—not merely with drugs that mask symptoms while often causing terrible side effects, but with treatments that address and correct the brain dysfunction underlying the dyslogical behavior.

- In every case, consider drugs as a last resort, not a first resort.

- Treat each dyslogical patient as a whole person, rather than as a single medical problem. In addition to evaluating brain function, evaluate every system—gastrointestinal, cardiovascular, endocrine, etc.—for evidence of abnormalities that can contribute to dysfunctional thinking and behavior.

- Do not confuse labels such as "conduct disorder," "schizophrenia," "depression," or "ADHD" for diagnoses. Instead, recognize that these are merely convenient labels for patterns of symptoms that arise from different insults to the brain.

- Use safe, effective, natural therapies that work with the body, rather than toxic, unnatural treatments that further disrupt homeostasis and, in the long run, generally exacerbate both brain and body dysfunction.

- Continue to try treatments until you find the ones that work—no matter how much trial and error is required.

- Keep an open mind! Expand your reading of the medical literature to include articles on the profound influence of nutrition and toxins on brain function.

- Treat parents as equal members of the treatment team. Never blame parents for their children's dyslogical behavior, unless you have concrete proof that they are at fault. And listen to the clues that parents give you. More often than not, these clues will point you to a diagnosis, a valuable treatment, or even a cure.

Action plan for the justice system

Too often, the dyslogical child who falls into a pattern of delinquent behavior never escapes. A delinquent youngster is all too likely to become a criminal adult, and his or her acts may easily escalate from petty theft or harassment to armed robbery, assault, or murder. "The record is discouraging," Allan Berman, M.D., once noted. "It is all the more frustrating since, at no point in this destructive cycle has the basic disability been addressed; not in school, not in the courts, not in rehabilitation institutions... The youngsters are treated either as criminals or as seriously psychopathological, with no attention directed toward the basic disability."[6] Tragically, few people in the system realize that those who least seem to deserve help may most need it.

When young delinquents do receive treatment, it's likely to come from social workers and psychologists who, following their training, blame social factors: poor parents, bad schools, poverty. It's true that a bad environment may push some children into crime, and a good environment might help some avoid trouble. But as I have shown in this book, even dyslogical children who come from good and loving families, as the vast majority do, are at higher risk than other children of ending up in juvenile hall, the courts, or the jails—not because of any failing on the part of their parents or society, but because of brain malfunction. Furthermore, unlike the biologically intact child who may respond to an improved home or school environment, the dyslogical criminal, with his real problem unsolved by these remedies, is likely to continue to escalate his criminal activities—to become the hard-core criminal that society fears most.

The most effective way to reduce the numbers of such "lost children" is to recognize that, in general, they suffer from *biological* abnormalities, to treat those abnormalities, and to undertake a massive effort to reduce or eliminate the environmental hazards that we know are associated with dyslogic-causing brain alterations. The consistent failure of expensive social and psychological programs to reduce crime, and the research showing that large percentages of juvenile criminals suffer from overt brain defects, are clear evidence that ignoring the biological roots of crime has been a costly mistake—for both the criminals and their victims.

How can we begin to undo this mistake? First, we can evaluate all young offenders for brain dysfunction, and when brain dysfunction is detected, we can immediately start to provide treatment that may help to prevent a first offender from becoming a repeat offender or a "lifer." The work of William Walsh (see Chapter 8) proves that even young delinquents considered to be incurable psychopaths can often be transformed into loving, law-abiding children, when mind-altering toxins are removed from their bodies and they receive adequate supplies of the nutrients needed to improve their thinking and behavior. The key word, however, is *young*; Walsh says that once children reach the later teen years, the snowballing effects of their biologically based dyslogic—drug abuse, alcohol abuse, poor self-image—can make it nearly impossible to turn their lives around.

In addition to identifying and treating brain dysfunction in young offenders, we can make the environment of dyslogical delinquents and criminals more healthful, not just for their bodies but also for their brains. The work (see Chapter 5) of Stephen Schoenthaler, and, more recently, Bernard Gesch, shows that simple dietary changes, relatively easy and inexpensive to implement, can dramatically reduce disordered behavior among prison populations. For young offenders, better brain function translates into an increased ability to understand the consequences of actions, an increased ability to learn academic skills, and enhanced empathy for the people around them—all of which can dramatically reduce the risk of repeat offenses.

Of course, treating brain dysfunction of young criminals, by identifying and addressing its causes, would cost society a significant amount of money up front. That cost, however, pales in comparison to the expense of repeatedly running dyslogical criminals through the courts and jail system, for years or even decades. It also pales in comparison to the cost of the sociological approaches used almost universally—and unsuccessfully—to "rehabilitate" prisoners. Diagnosing, treating, and curing the brain dysfunction of a young criminal might cost as much as $5000 or $10,000. If the same criminal spends the next 25 years in and out of courtrooms, correctional centers, and prisons, undergoing endless courses of unsuccessful rehabilitation, the tab will easily be 10, 20, or even 50 times higher. (The average cost in

2003 of incarcerating a juvenile for a *single year* was between $35,000 and $64,000.)[7] More important, stopping dyslogic-caused delinquency before it escalates into adult criminality will protect the lives and well-being of thousands of innocent Americans. While there is much controversy over the sentencing and punishment of criminals, there should be no controversy at all over the fact that it is preferable to prevent criminal acts, and the grief, turmoil, and destruction they cause, in the first place.

Treating current offenders and at-risk children, however, is just part of the solution to the problem of dyslogic-based criminality. In addition, it is imperative that we encourage more scientific investigation into the biological causes of delinquency and criminality, rather than shying away from such research out of misplaced concern about being politically incorrect (see Chapter 2). Notes Judge Richard L. Nygaard, of the United States Court of Appeals for the Third Circuit, "The search for truth about behavior may lead us to facts about nutrition, neurotransmitters, toxins, testosterone levels, brain damage, genes and a host of other variables hitherto unexamined, that explain behavior; hence may explain crime."[8] These explanations, he says, could move us far closer to establishing a judicial system that can turn at-risk children away from lives of crime, and reduce the rates of repeating offenses by those already convicted.

Unfortunately, the justice system, much like the medical system, is adamantly resistant to change. Says Nygaard:

> Penology is about mental health, but our sentencing policy pays little attention to the medical, biological or social sciences. Correction of criminal offenders is about change, but our penal system is content with punishment alone. Although science has much to tell law, law is not listening.

But if enough individuals working within the justice system speak out—from lawyers and judges to prison wardens, parole officers, and medical personnel within our correctional facilities—their voices will, eventually, be heard. When that happens, both offenders and the society that must deal with them will be far better off.

SUMMARY: ACTION PLAN FOR JUDGES, PRISON
WARDENS, PROBATION OFFICERS, AND OTHER
MEMBERS OF THE JUSTICE SYSTEM

- Acknowledge the failure of sociological attempts at
rehabilitating offenders, and be open minded about
seeking more effective alternatives.

- Encourage the justice system to recognize that
delinquent or criminal behavior frequently stems from
a dysfunctional brain, and that treating the brain
dysfunction can reduce antisocial behavior and
dramatically lower rates of recidivism.

- Provide in-depth medical screening for all offenders
and, in particular, children, teens, and young adults.
Early treatment of dyslogic is the most effective
treatment.

- Provide a healthful diet to incarcerated offenders, to
aid in correcting the nutritional deficiencies that often
contribute to dyslogical or dangerous behavior.

- Promote further scientific research into biological
causes of, and biomedical treatments for, criminal and
delinquent behavior.

The Action Plan I've outlined constitutes an ambitious agenda that
requires the combined intelligence, commitment, and resources of
millions of Americans: parents, teachers, principals, counselors,
doctors, judges, and law enforcement professionals. But the results, as
the examples I've cited in this book amply demonstrate, are well worth
the effort. Imagine a massive drop in the numbers of children who turn
to hateful, hurtful, criminal behavior. Imagine classrooms where
students, rather than being drugged into submission, behave and learn
and enjoy their lives. Imagine medical care that cures dyslogic, rather
than adding to its symptoms with toxic drugs or subjecting its victims
(and their families) to hours of futile psychotherapy. And, if you're the
parent of a dyslogical child, imagine seeing that child improve every

day—becoming happier, healthier, more joyful, less aggressive, less depressed, less oppositional, less frightening. Imagine that instead of fearing what the next day will bring, you can look forward to your child's future, and once again dream and plan.

These are not impossible goals. I know, because I know many parents and professionals who have accomplished them. I can't promise a miracle for every dyslogical child, but I can promise that the majority of parents and professionals who implement the ideas I've outlined will see improvements in dyslogical children that they once thought were unattainable.

Unfortunately, if you choose to implement these approaches, you are likely to encounter stiff opposition from entrenched medical and educational interests. A long-ago article in the *Journal of the American Medical Association*, by James and Jean Goodwin, referred to this phenomenon as "The Tomato Effect." The authors noted that the tomato was discovered in the New World, and was brought back to Spain and Italy where by the year 1560 it had become a staple of the European diet. Strangely, however, very few people in North America would even consider eating tomatoes; since tomatoes belong to the nightshade family, people in America were advised that they were poisonous. It seemed to make no difference to the people in North America that the Spanish and Italians ate large quantities of tomatoes without being poisoned. The Goodwins observed, "Not until 1820, when Robert Gibbon Johnson ate a tomato on the steps of the courthouse of Salem, New Jersey, and survived, did the people of America begin, grudgingly, we suspect, to consume tomatoes."[9]

"Don't bother me with facts, my mind is made up"—it was true then, and it is true today. The Goodwins went on to point out that many highly efficacious therapies have been rejected and repudiated by the medical authorities of the time, for reasons as irrational as those that caused the rejection of tomatoes for several centuries. For instance:

- From 1900 to 1950, no leading medical textbook or medical article on rheumatoid arthritis mentioned aspirin as a treatment for the disorder, although the benefits of this treatment were known.

- The benefits of lithium—one of the few "miracle drugs" that has actually lived up to the name—were discovered in the 1940s, but as late as 1958 the *Pharmacological Basis of Therapeutics*, a major reference work, stated that "the lithium ion has no therapeutic applications and, so far as is known, no biological function."[10]

- The doctors who discovered that scurvy and pellagra stemmed from vitamin deficiencies were ostracized by other physicians.

- The doctor who discovered that most ulcers stemmed from bacterial infection (and not from stress, as once believed) was denied the right to speak at medical conventions and was shunned by his colleagues until his theory was proven beyond any doubt.

- The doctors who first discovered that high doses of folic acid helped to prevent neural tube defects in pregnant women were ignored for decades, while tens of thousands of babies suffered or died needlessly.

- Kilmer McCully discovered in the 1960s that deficiencies of vitamin B6, vitamin B12, and folic acid were linked to heart disease. Today, mainstream doctors routinely prescribe these nutrients to lower dangerous homocysteine levels and protect the cardiovascular system. Yet McCully's work was scorned by his colleagues at Harvard, and went unnoticed by the medical profession for decades.

Similarly, the most safe and effective methods of treating dyslogic have until recently been victims of the "Tomato Effect." No amount of research—and the research continues to mount—can convince some skeptics that these therapies have value.

Fortunately, such chronically skeptical "authorities" are no longer able to prevent knowledge from reaching the people who need to see it. Only a few decades ago, medical information resided primarily in textbooks and journals read almost solely by doctors. Now, this information is available to anyone with an Internet connection or a library card, and parent groups are springing up everywhere to spread the word about nutritional interventions, detoxification treatments, and other effective strategies for treating dyslogic. Every day, open-minded parents and professionals, in the tradition of the tomato-tasting Johnson, are announcing that they have tried the approaches I advocate, and have discovered that these approaches do indeed work.

We hope that you will join these modern-day Robert Gibbon Johnsons, and try the safe, rational approaches that this book outlines. My colleagues and I believe that, when you do, you will discover that they are infinitely more effective than the drug treatments and psychotherapy that the mainstream medical community touts. When you do, please spread the word—because it is up to you, the parents and professionals who care about dyslogical children, to let others know that there is help and hope. Together, we can conquer dyslogic, with the help of the educational, legal, and educational communities—and in doing so, we can create a better future for ourselves, our children, and countless generations to come.

Notes

1 Personal communication.

2 "Impact of Healing Foods on Learning and Behavior: Five Year Study." DVD, produced by Natural Ovens Bakery, Inc., P.O. Box 730, Manitowoc, WI 54221, October 2004.

3 Simontacchi, C. (2000) *The Crazy Makers*. New York: Jeremy P. Tarcher/Putnam, pp.147–9.

4 Cited in M. Maser (2000) "Failing kids with fast foods in the cafeteria." *Georgia Straight*, February. Available at www.channel1media.com/Ramona/georgia.html (accessed 4 october 2007).

5 "Health movement has school cafeterias in a food fight," *USA Today*, August 21, 2005.

6 Berman, A. "Delinquents are disabled," paper presented to the Youth in Trouble Symposium, Dallas, Texas, 2 May 1974.

7 ACLU Fact Sheet on the Juvenile Justice System, July 5, 1996.

8 Nygaard, R.L. (2000) *Sentencing as I See It*. Incline Village, Nevada: Copperhouse Publishing Company.

9 Goodwin, J.S. and Goodwin, J.M. (1984) "The tomato effect: Rejection of highly efficacious therapies." *Journal of the American Medical Association 251*, 18, 2387–90.

10 Diamond, E. (1969) "Lithium vs. mental illness." *New York Times Magazine*, January 12.

Subject Index

Author Index